THE POETIC

LOVE

OF GOD

By

Calvin (Cal) Alford

Hidden Manna Publications
P.O. Box 3572
Oldtown, ID. 83822

The Poetic Love of God
Copyright © 2018 by Calvin Alford

ISBN: 978-0-9864066-6-9

Cover Design: Pam Wester

Printed in the USA

The views expressed in this work are solely those of the author and do not necessarily reflect the views of the publisher, and the publisher hereby disclaims any responsibility for them.

Except where otherwise indicated, all Scriptures in this book were based on the King James Version.

Table of Contents

INTRODUCTION

I want to introduce you to the poetry of Calvin (Cal) Alford. I became aware of Cal and his poetry when I attended the same church as he. It was there that I first became acquainted with his poems.

Cal would often read one of his poems after our time of worship. He has always given the credit for the poems he has written to heavenly inspiration. At the end of one of his poems, he penned these words, "It has been said by someone, I should write a book, and maybe someday I will. Then it occurred to me, the one who set me free, Jesus, already wrote the book." However, there is a passion burning in Calvin to share his gift. He actually put some of his poems into five different books, one wire bound and some stapled, which he had handed out to all who readily received them. He had attempted to find someone who would publish them, but was met with false promises and closed doors.

Clearly, it has been Cal's aspiration to share these poems with others as a means of blessing their souls while causing their spirits to soar, ever desirous in bringing glory to the real inspiration behind his writings, his Creator, Redeemer, and God.

This book includes his five books of poems along with some new additions. In one of his books, he recorded some of his thoughts about the inspiration behind his poems. These notations and thoughts have been clearly noted and put in a separate section entitled, "Personal Notations and Thoughts," beginning on page 147 of this book for further edification of the reader.

Rayola Kelley
Publisher

I've Seen Seen Jesus

Book One

CLOSER TO GOD

There are still some hills to climb.
Thank you Lord for giving us extra time.

Lord, you are not willing that any are lost
Thank you Lord for paying all that it cost.

The first will be last and the last will be first.
Some will be blessed, yet still some will be cursed.

Some will be forgiven, when they come closer to thee.
Some will be forgiven; some can yet be set free.

We all need to come closer to God: that is what I've heard.
Jesus is waiting to save you, our Holy Living Word.

Jesus is the Author and Finisher of our faith, who gave us hope.
No other was able to save us or to throw us a rope.

Jesus endured the cross, despising the shame,
Sitting at the right hand of the Father, building us a new name.

CLEAN FEET

Walking in the garden, there's roses that have thorns.
Walking with Jesus my Savior, He has taken away the devil's horns.

Walking in the mountains with storm clouds rolling overhead.
Walking with Jesus means our sinful nature is now dead.

Walking in the valley, crossing raging rivers and shallow streams.
Walking with Jesus, He has given me my fondest dreams.

Walking in the shadows, playing games with darkness at its post.
Jesus sent the Comforter, there is safety in the Holy Ghost.

If we have sickness in our bodies, we need Jesus in our head.
With Jesus in charge, we will have healing instead.

Walking in the world's dirt, we get dust upon our shoes.
Jesus came to wash our feet, with Jesus we can't lose.

Jesus said if you don't let me wash your feet you have no part with me.
Now that Jesus has rolled the clouds away, God's glory sets us free.

ON GOD'S HIGHWAY

We can count on Jesus, when we are on the road.
We can count on Jesus, when burdens weigh a heavy load.

We can count on Jesus, when we are happy or sad.
We can count on Jesus, when times are good or bad.

Now that we know Jesus, the worst is not that bad.
Now that we know Jesus, we are looking at better times then we've
ever had.

Although time is short, we have an eternity.
Although time is short, it doesn't matter,
If you know Jesus personally.

Jesus went on ahead, nothing stands in our way.
Jesus is coming, look up oh happy day.

DON'T LOOK BACK

With our past forgiven, we must not hang onto what is rotten.
With the Lord in our future the past is forgotten.

We must not look back, with longing in our hearts to the past.
We must not go back to take anything out of our house that won't last.

The things that we have, must not have us too.
Let go of the past to freedom is what we must do.

Send out only good, and receive only the same.
Do good unto others only in Jesus' name.

Taking one day at a time, trusting in God for the best,
Keeping our eyes on Jesus, striving to enter God's rest.

Jesus withheld nothing, He flung open the door.
Don't withhold from others the love that they long for.

Jesus King of kings, He is worthy to wear the crown.
Jesus breached Satan's walls and tore them all down.

Those that follow Satan will be bound and thrown into darkness,
Hate will be their reward.
Jesus said He is building the faithful a mansion,
Without Jesus the cost we could not afford.

FAITHFUL HEART

In lonely places God walks with the faithful heart.
When Jesus walks with us, we can be sure of victory from the start.

In times of sadness, we are not alone God loves the faithful heart.
If we love Jesus, He will never leave us; His love will set us apart.

When we praise God with gladness, no need for sadness,
His love heals the faithful heart.
With Jesus guiding the horse we are riding, He is always before the cart.

When the mind is filled, worry starts to build,
Remember God will save the faithful heart.

When you're lost in the crowd with the noise getting loud,
God will not forget.
You will not be left in the pit, if you keep a faithful heart.

If our faith starts to waiver, we need to seek God's favor.
God has the faithful heart.

If we don't let ourselves stray, everything is ok.
Our God is the faithful heart.

Jesus wants you to know, there is no place you can go.
That He can't save you, He is the faithful heart.

GOD'S HOUSE

The house that God built can be easy to be.
The walls and the ceiling, God built like a tree.

The roots run deep, they are nourished by God.
The roots are growing, deep in the sod.

The winds are blowing, and moving the branches around.
Those that love Jesus bend, not making a sound.

We love you forever Jesus, Your love forever will be.
Come Holy Spirit move the branches of this tree.

With no love for Jesus, and strong winds start to blow.
Those branches will break and be covered by snow.

The trees all turn green, Jesus has opened the door.
When winter is over and spring comes once more.

Up towards heaven, new life out of darkness shoots.
The trees again grow with new life from the roots.

GOING FISHING
WITH JESUS

I'm going fishing with Jesus; we are not going to let the big ones get away.
I'm going fishing with Jesus; He is coming to my house to stay.

I'm going fishing with Jesus; He tells me we are going to catch men.
I'm going fishing with Jesus; I'm taking my ballpoint pen.

Jesus said I don't need to take anything with me, Jesus is everything I need.
I'm going fishing with Jesus; we are going to plant some seed.

Jesus is everything we need; His Spirit gives us new birth.
God is going to give us a harvest that stretches to the end of the earth.

Jesus said He loves me, after hearing that, how can I help but be delighted.
I'm going fishing with Jesus: I'm so happy I'm getting quite a bit excited.

Let's all go fishing with Jesus; Jesus loves to show us how.
Jesus is coming to your house, listen, Jesus is calling you now.

No matter how little or big you are, there is room in Jesus' boat.
Jesus walked on water; Jesus is able to keep us afloat.

FONDEST MOMENTS

I may only be a fisherman that was sent out by Jesus to fish.
God's grace is sufficient for me, I have my fondest wish.

It seems just like a dream, yet it is very true.
Jesus has given me life, has He also given life to you?

What God gave, He will never take away.
If we hang unto love, everything is going to be okay.

You can trust the One that loves you more than His own life you see.
Jesus gave up His life for all of us, and said, "Forgive them," as He
was hanging on the tree.

Jesus felt alone, His Father had turned away.
Our sins were taken by Jesus, upon that dark day.

God has a promise for those that ask to be forgiven.
For those that are truly sorry for the way we have been livin'.

FORGIVEN

Twelve hours of darkness, can bring on the day.
Twelve minutes with Jesus, can bring love to stay.

Twelve months of prayer, is only one year,
Twelve days of repentance, can alleviate fear.

Saying Jesus I'm sorry on one's knees, is how to make amends.
Twelve disciples of Jesus, all but one, became His close friends.

God is no respecter of persons, He's always true.
Don't worry what people think, they don't have a clue.

Minutes and hours, time is marching along.
Jesus is number one, I'm singing His song.

17

You might as well give up, God's going to win.
God's got your number; you can't hide your sin.

If we want to be Jesus' very closest friend,
We must do good to our enemies right to the end.

BEST FRIEND

If you would lift your neighbor
Up out of servitude,
Treat Him with kindness
When He is very rude.

Smile at him and tell him
To have a nice day.
And when you are in your prayer closet,
Get on your knees and pray.

Do what you can to help him
To walk in light along the way.
And chase away the darkness
That threatens to ruin his day.

If he has things that are broken,
That he needs to mend.
Tell Him about Jesus,
Your very special friend.

Now when you are happy,
Go and plant a little seed.
And when it is time to harvest,
It will be just what you need.

Calvin Alford

FULL PARDON

We are God's children conceived by the love of God.
Walking after Jesus, Jesus plants new life in the sod.

Sending love to those who are called, the storm cloud's rolled away.
Jesus is the answer, better times, there's coming a new day.

If we love and trust in Jesus, that day is already here.
Jesus is the answer; His love quiets hate and fear.

There is a time for sorrow, yet Jesus will wipe away each tear.
Jesus is the answer; His love takes away the child's fear.

For God's praise and glory, the prayers of God's children go up to heaven's gardens.
God is calling His children home; His plan for His children is full pardons.

NEW LIFE

The man who loves His life will lose it or,
He can give it up and God will use it.

Unless a single seed dies it remains only one little seed,
The life given for others fill many a need.

When we give up our old life and let the Spirit of Jesus renew,
New life will spring up in the things that we do.

GET BEHIND ME SATAN

Satan you've kicked my dog till it won't hunt no more.
You've begin to make me just a little sore.

Satan you've jumped in my pond and muddied my water.
Now you tell me you want to marry my daughter.

Satan you've walked all over the roses in my garden.
Say what, you won't even say I beg your pardon!

You've taken the hairs off of my head,
You've given me a stone instead of bread.

You've lied to me for the very last time.
I'm not going to give you even one more dime.

Satan the things you want me to do aren't even fun.
Get behind me Satan, Jesus is going to make you run.

Satan I'm throwing you out of my house now.
That's the last time you're stealing milk from my cow.

LAST HOUR

Lord build in me a strong heart filled with your power.
Give me strength to do the work until the very last hour.

Lord sweep all the darkness out of me, fill me with Your light of love.
Fill my heart with your things that come from up above.

Take for us Lord the things of this world that fill us with hate.
Oh please Lord do this before it becomes too late.

Take all the things that separate us from you.
Please build a wall around us that can't be broken through.

Lord show us where your will lies within us all,
So we may stand up straight and tall.

Give your hand to us of the things you are giving,
So we may lead others where your people are living.

BRIDGES

Be careful what bridges you burn in your life.
Be good to the woman that you call your wife.

Be good to the man that stands beside you.
Don't burn all your bridges, before life is through.

Bridges bring people together that are a long ways away.
Let's all stand together on Judgment Day.

Don't burn that bridge until we all get to the other side.
Jesus is your Savior from Him you can't hide.

There is one bridge that some have not crossed.
God is not willing that any are lost.

THE ANSWER

If you want answers when you pray,
Walk close to Jesus every day.

If you have lots of fences to mend,
Treat Jesus like your best friend.

If you see others that have a need,
Don't let your heart be ruled by greed.

Give to Jesus all the glory.
Then you will know the rest of the story.

You only need to read the end of the book.
The Holy Spirit will give you the answer when you look.

Put a smile on your face.
Take Jesus with you every place.

The answer is right in front of you.
Jesus is the answer, I thought you knew.

GOD'S MOUNTAIN

Master hide me please, when I get on my knees,
Master let me sit at your feet, spiritual food yet to eat.

Fear is a shadow of the enemy passing by, this is fear.
Blackness, it is hard to fear darkness with Jesus walking near.

Jesus is light, He won't let darkness go straight through. He is light.
With Jesus with us there is no darkness, no night.

When we get to heaven, no more dark and lonely mountains to climb.
We will be at the top of God's mountain in plenty of time.

At the top of God's mountain, the pain won't matter anymore.
Jesus is with us, forever, like the eagle we're going to soar.

ALTHOUGH WE MAY APPEAR

Although we may appear to be at the end of our rope,
In Jesus, there is no end to our hope.

Although it may appear that we haven't got a prayer,
There is nothing to worry about because Jesus is there.

Although we appear to be standing alone in the dark,
Jesus is with us, it's a walk in the park.

We can have victory day after day,
If we trust in Jesus to carry us all the way.

If we keep the promise of God in our heart,
The things of the world won't be able to tear us apart.

If you have a problem that is too big for you,
Give it to Jesus, He knows what to do.

HEAVEN'S BREAD

We are on our way towards home right now.
Jesus showed us the way to get there wow!

With Jesus already guarding the home front.
It's time to follow; we've found what we hunt.

The path is much brighter now.
Since our blessed Savior showed us how.

We have been traveling on the way.
It's given much meaning to our day.

Some of the way has been a surprise.
It's okay nothing gets past Jesus' eyes.

We have yet a long way to travel.
Only God knows how life will unravel.

Jesus went on to make ready what's ahead.
He has left the Comforter, we live on heaven's bread.

Jesus left His name; He has staked us out a claim.

Jesus is waiting for us at heaven's gate.
For His bride, we must not be late.

BORN AGAIN

I heard Jesus speak to me.
He opened my eyes, I began to see.

I heard Jesus' voice as others spoke.
I realized I was spiritually broke.

When I saw others better than I,
Jesus said, "In eternity we will not die."

Jesus said, "When you know me as I have always known you,
In your heart you have become a Jew."

Now, I have been born again.
Jesus has saved me from all my sin.

Jesus said, "As I have been lifted up on the tree,
Very soon you will be in Paradise with me."

Jesus said He loves me and He loves you,
Now what is important is that we love Jesus, too.

I FOUND LOVE

Of all that my Jesus has given me,
Of all that the thing in the world I see.

Of all that comes to my limited mind,
My Jesus is still just one of a kind.

No need for anyone to be jealous of me, Lord.
If we all draw closer to Jesus in one accord.

Of all that Jesus has given to me,
Jesus is the one that holds the key.

It seems like it was only yesterday,
That Jesus sent me on my way.

Jesus put in our hearts love of God's own kind.
If you are looking for love, Jesus is the One you will find.

THE END OF THE TRAIL

Thank you, Jesus, for speaking to me,
When I was in darkness, unable to see.

I wandered all over, unable to say,
For what reason did I get up today.

Thank you, Jesus, for speaking to me,
I was blind, and the truth set me free.

All I gave you was trouble and pain,
And you gave me the soft latter rain.

Please, Jesus, don't let my eyesight fail,
I want to follow you to the end of the trail.

FAITH, HOPE, AND LOVE

Trust only God in the things you hear.
In what man says, have no fear.

Trust in God in the things you see.
Man without God can never be free.

With your faith in Jesus firmly in place,
You will be in front at the end of the race.

The hope in Jesus that you have right now,
Is a sure thing, put your hand to the plow.

The greatest is love, there is no doubt.
God is love, that's what it's all about.

GOD'S IMAGE

We all can put a smile on our face.
We all are in the world in the same race.

We all can know and love each other.
We are father, mother, sister, brother.

This poem can go on to the end of time.
God put us in harmony, we just seem to rhyme.

Everyone seems to fit, everyone has their place.
Even if I added to this poem the whole human race.

You can take any name and put it right here.
They would soon fit right in, you need have no fear.

Jesus said He would pour out His Spirit on the whole human race.
If you look closely you will see Jesus in everyone's face.

It does not matter, we cannot deny it.
We are made in God's image, we cannot defy it.

Jesus Christ is totally fair.
Like it or not, we make a pretty good pair.

We are all one family, In Jesus we are one.
Praise God, give Him glory, this can even be fun.

WHO IS IN CHARGE

Did you want to be in charge, whatever the cost?
And now that you are looked up to, do you feel completely lost?

Do you say, "I wish Jesus would help me out a bit?
Well, don't get discouraged, don't give up and quit.

The answer is so simple; here is what you need to do.
Ask Jesus to take charge, and He will carry you.

Ask Jesus to go with you as you are on your way to work along the road.
Introduce those you meet to Jesus, it will lighten up their load.

All the angels in heaven will recognize it really is true,
Jesus has always been in charge, it never really was you.

OVER THE HILL

One if by me, two if by you.
Put us together, in Jesus brand new.

Let us agree; Jesus is the one we belong to.
Let us agree; Jesus is the one we follow in the things that we do.

In Jesus we are first, in line we are last.
Our faith in the world has already been cast.

When we followed in the world, as blind as a bat.
Now we walk in the light, Jesus gives us sight where we are at.

Longing to walk close to our Savior and Lord.
All the treasures of heaven in our heart we have stored,

When we work to go forward, we can't stand still.
With love for each other, we will walk together over the hill.

Jesus paid the price, Jesus paid the bill.
Jesus wants us to help each other get over the hill.

MOUNTAIN

Forty years but who's counting,
One more trip around the mountain.

One more year without drinking from the Fountain of Life.
It's time that I make peace from all my strife.

One more year but who's counting,
Without drinking from God's fountain.

With all the time I have wasted,
So many things I could have tasted.

I may still have time if I hurry,
If I don't stop and begin to worry.

Jesus said if you ask to be forgiven,
You can get down to real livin'.

When God forgives you, it's just as if you sinned never.
You take the time that you have wasted, subtract that from forever.

JESUS IS THE FUTURE

Don't fear the enemy, fear God only, He is loving and kind.
Jesus loves us more than anyone else you can find.

There is no fear in heaven, not even a lie will enter there.
If we belong to Jesus we will have brothers and sisters that care.

Jesus said if we agree with Him we are His brothers, sisters, and mother.
There is strength in numbers, if we will agree with Jesus and each other.

If we follow after Jesus, in the way that God goes.
We will all be on the same page in the Book of Life that flows.

Read your Bible every day, live the words that are printed there.
Everyone needs to follow Jesus, with their cross to bear.

In the pages of the Bible, are the words that bring life in full bloom.
In the arms of God's blessings, for all of us there's room.

If we truly love Jesus in understanding we have come far,
In the pages of the Bible, Jesus is the Bright and Morning Star.

If we study God's Word with our heart we will have what we seek.
The evidence of the Holy Spirit is that everyone understands what we speak.

If we don't accept the evil the enemy begins to spout.
Pressure backs up on the one that sends it out.

No more indecision when God fills us from His throne above.
Jesus is the doorway into a bright future filled with love.

MUSIC IS MEDICINE

Music is medicine that heals from the heart inside.
Music is medicine that takes away hateful pride.

Music is medicine that cries out for God's touch.
Music is medicine that my heart cries out for this much.

Music is medicine that I want to sing and dance before the Lord.
Please join in we will all sing praises in one accord.

Music is medicine, bow down and pray, Jesus heal my body and soul.
Music is medicine Jesus please heal me and make me whole.

Jesus please come by here and heal me.
Music is medicine, more real than we can see.

Here I am Lord, mold me and make me new.
God let this be a prayer and a love letter to you.

Our desire is to follow after and be a reflection and dedication too.
We are your lump of clay Lord, we only want to follow you.

NO FEAR

I have lovely butterflies inside of me.
Thank you Jesus for hearing my plea.

I want to walk in the places that Jesus walks.
I want to talk just like my Jesus talks.

I want to see the world as Jesus sees.
I know Jesus has the answer, Jesus holds the keys.

In the hands of Jesus there is healing for us all.
In the hands of Jesus He will not let us fall.

God's banner over us is love, and no matter what happens from here,
There is nothing for us to worry about; Jesus has separated us from
fear.

I'm going to put my money in the Savior's bank.
I know not to trust in the Titanic, because it sank.

I'm going to trust Jesus; I know He walked on the water all alone.
Jesus has got your number, Jesus is calling, answer your phone.

God's children have been scattered world over, no more time to roam.
God is calling His children; it's time to come on home.

I'M NOT CRAZY

Please listen closely to what Jesus said.
Don't look for Jesus among the dead.

Please listen closely to what Jesus said.
For you and me Jesus' blood was shed.

Please hear the words that Jesus speaks.
We have a home above lofty peaks.

Jesus promised and we can trust.
If we want to get to heaven, Jesus is a must.

I'm not worried, everything is okay.
We will all see Jesus upon that day.

Paul said I'm not crazy as you suppose or you believe.
I'm going to tell you about my Lord before I leave.

WE TOO WILL KNOW

The light will dance on the waters of life,
The song of the angels, God gave man a wife.

Walking with Jesus makes all burdens light.
Jesus walked on the water, His robe of pure white.

Our Father in heaven looks down on His lamb's pastures of green.
Jesus washed His disciple's feet, He makes all that He touches pure
and clean.

Alone in the wilderness Jesus fasted, yet did no sin.
Think back to the Garden where all this did begin.

Mom and Daddy went to heaven not long ago.
When we all get to heaven, then we too will know.

31

JESUS THE VERY BEST

Along comes spring in the beginning of life's struggles.
Along comes spring in mother's arms, it's times of snuggles.

In the spring of life we are nursed on milk and gentle training.
With mother's love, and father's love, as babies we hardly notice when it's raining.

In the summer time of life, solid food needs to be eaten to be healthy.
We can choose life and living in the light in all things of God become wealthy.

Summertime of life we learn about love that sometimes comes out in giggles.
God loved us first, if we feel loved when we are young it can come out in wiggles.

When fall comes into one's life the beauty and love of God is all around.
When Jesus makes His love known as King of kings was when Jesus was crowned.

When winter time in life comes this can be the very best.
That is if we know Jesus we can stop worrying about all the rest.

Jesus went to the cross, so we would not fail.
Jesus said, "Put your hand in mine, feel the marks of the nail."

LAMP GLOW

God is calling His children; it's time to come on home now.
Jesus lit the path to where every knee shall bow.

If you have Jesus in your life, turn the darkness inside out till nothing is
left but light.
When in the light you won't look back into the pitch blackness of the
dark of night.

In the place where Jesus takes you there is never any night.
There is nothing to fear from darkness when Jesus has called you to
the light.

When Jesus fills your life with truth there isn't any reason to hide.
Jesus will lighten your burdens; He will stay close by your side.

You will never have to say good-by forever to the things that you hold
dear.
If you ask God with all your heart to make the world free from fear.

When things seem the darkest it's almost dawn.
The light will soon break forth with day coming on.

Jesus is in the hearts of the people that follow Him.
Jesus gives gifts to the ones that let not their lamps grow dim.

LIGHT OF TRUE NORTH

Jesus is making us a home, it's not too far.
Jesus is guiding us home, our Bright Morning Star.

God's will is that we follow Jesus' example.
The good we see on earth is only a sample.

God gives to those that love Him, God strengthens those that care.
God gives to those wisdom that stand fast and give to others a share.

There is no more tomorrow in the light of today.
Before tomorrow comes it's filled up when we pray.

When the sun is sinking low, the light fades away.
When the light comes again, Jesus fills it with day.

Jesus is the greatest light ever sent to the earth.
Jesus is the Bright and Morning Star of new birth.

Once we were searching, for Jesus the greatest around.
Once we were searching now we have been found.

God said, "Let there be light," and the light shined fourth.
If you are following Jesus, set your compass true north.

MORE THAN BEANS

The devil made me bitter, and God made me better.
The devil got me lost, Jesus He paid the cost.

The devil sold me out, my Jesus turned me about.
The devil made me blind, my Jesus healed my mind.

The devil said, "It's warm come on down," Jesus said, "I have for you a
crown."
The devil has earned furnaces heat, the devil is under Jesus' feet.

If we say, "Heavenly Father forgive us our sin,"
We will get more than beans, that's when we win.

Looking to see Jesus as we get closer still.
Helping each other to climb up the hill.

PRIESTHOOD

The object of all priesthood is to bring to God in spiritual communion.
Jesus the High Priest, the Mediator of the union.

Father God is pleased with Jesus it is true.
If you belong to Jesus, He is pleased with you too.

God sees us thru the blood of Jesus that we are covered by.
Following Jesus to the top, no limit how high.

Although my eyesight is getting dim.
Father God sees all, no limits on Him.

God has promised to subdue all our sins.
If God is in your life, God always wins.

The Lord promised to cause us to walk holy, Jesus removed the veil.
What is impossible for man, God does without fail.

I will not hang onto the regret of the past.
Jesus is with me, I'm home at last.

THE REST OF THE STORY

Tears in the eyes, pain in the heart,
The end of the wicked was for sure from the start.

The wicked can't continue; their end is assured.
It is all recorded down in the pages of God's Word.

The wicked have risen up for their time here on earth.
Love they have rejected, instead they have chosen the curse.

The clock is ticking; it's almost time to hold court.
With their time running out, for the wicked, time is getting short.

The Word of the Lord is what true believers fear.
The sound of the call to battle can be heard coming near.

The wicked man if all he gives is hate,
Death is for certain to be waiting as he reaches home plate.

If our life is in Christ, grounded in the Spirit,
Satan and his angels can't come anywhere near it.

There is power from God to be healed by His power for His glory.
What those that were chosen by Jesus heard was, "the rest of the story."

RESTORING GRACE

The wife that is playing with Satan: the husband that is running after other gods.
As husbands and wives we are in trouble, without Jesus it is against all odds.

God wants the latter part of our lives to be better than the first.
When we learn to grow up, give help to others, we have overcome the worst.

Do you see Jesus coming and restoring and rebuilding everything?
Peace, joy, lands relationships, and hope that's what love can bring.

In God's field plant seed with care it will conceive.
We become what we spend our time on; Jesus is the One we believe.

Focus on all the wondrous things that God can do.
Don't waste time without God, on what is impossible for you.

The question is will we trust in Jesus, pray in faith; Jesus saved the day.
The truth is Jesus is the only way.

Jesus knows all our secrets, He knows we flunked the test.
God said He was giving us an "A" because it is the best.

SPIRITUAL BATTLE

Call others to battle the enemy is lost in the fact of eternity.
You are a commander in God's army sent forth, all see victory.

Jesus is seeking a few good people
To place on the Church He is building: a steeple.
The lead position out of the Bible, held by the pastor,
A solid foundation is laid by Jesus our Master.

When it's time to sail into the deep, on route to that distant shore,
Jesus does not want us to worry if we land and find ourselves at war.

The battle belongs to God, keep your eyes locked on the Master.
Jesus will lead us through the storms of life till we come to greener
pastures.

THE FUTURE

Faith and trust in Jesus is it reality of what is unseen?
If we wash our hands with care then we believe our hands to be clean.

Jesus walked on water, knowing His Father does miracles in facts.
There is power in faith, Jesus leaves no doubt, nothing lacks.

There is no one else we need to put our trust in.
Jesus has overcome all things, destroying the power of sin.

Apologies can carry sorrow for the things one has done.
Yet in the morning light there is the victory Jesus has won.

One stands on the land, there is no more sea.
Every eye will see Jesus, praising God we are free.

The Alpha and the Omega, the Beginning and the End,
Our God holds the future that is just around the bend.

We only have eternity to praise God it's true.
Although sometimes we might falter, God never gave up on you.

THE QUICK AND THE DEAD

Jesus is the savior of us all. Trust that God can.
Don't worry faithful believer, for God has a plan.

Our job is to make sure, all have heard about the fairness of love.
Walk only in the light that shines from Father God's throne above.

My advice to you, if you have people you know that make you grieve,
Be sure you tell them of the blessing of Jesus before you leave.

Looking at the tallest mountains that exist here on earth,
God knew our whole story, before He gave us new birth.

Everyone will see Christ on the day that has been chosen.
Jesus can melt all our loved ones, even if their hearts have been frozen.

THRONS AMONGST ROSES

Mercies of God in service of love's holiness each hour,
Blessings are falling, transformed by renewing love and power.

Father God measures faith by Jesus Christ only, we have no boast at all.
Grace is sent by Jesus to the many parts of His Body, blessings fall.

Thorns stand amongst the roses this is a fact.
When Jesus calls us to serve Him, let's make sure our lamp oil is packed.

Let's give to those in need, let's plant a little seed.

Let's carry with us the things that are needed most.
Love above all, kindness in full measure, hope from coast to coast.

Jesus gives the water of life so that thirst will not return.
Let's give the hand of Jesus, so that others can learn.

Let's pray for all the soldiers in the battle on distant shore.
Let's pray for the Iraqi people and that hostilities are no more.

GOD LOVES EVERYONE

What would you give up for Jesus for the life He gave for you?
There isn't anything, there is nothing we can do.

Jesus said, "What you do to the least of these, you do to me."
A coat, or shoes, or anything, it must be given free.

Jesus paid a higher price than we could ever pay.
If we give our life to Jesus, we'll have treasure on judgment day.

Not because of anything that we could ever do,
But because of what Jesus was already going to do.

If we give all we have to Jesus, it would be the right thing to do.
Yet, it would not come close to what Jesus has given you.

Because He loves His enemies, as He loves everyone,
You cannot out give God, for He gave us His Son.

THANKFULNESS

Thank you Lord for showing the weakness we see.
Thank you Lord for making us what you want us to be.

Lord make our eyes clear, so the ball we won't fumble.
Lord don't let us to cause anyone else to stumble.

Thank you Lord for holding us by the hand.
Thank you Lord for not letting us put our heads in the sand.

Thank you Lord for the peace, filled with the joy of winning.
Thank you Lord for guiding us from the time of our beginning.

Thank you Lord for showing us beauty, and thankfulness.
Thank you Lord for taking us thru the wilderness.

Thank you, Lord for you encouragement that makes us strong.
Thank you, Lord for friends that show us when we are wrong.

When we come home, Lord let not any lose their sight.
When we come home, Lord let us be all clothed in white.

NO OTHER NAME

I want to sit and learn at Jesus' feet.
My precious Savior I want you to meet.

I love to see my grandchildren grow.
I'm very happy when my Jesus they know.

Jesus has known us from the beginning of time and forever.
Jesus loves us, even if we know Him not, or loved Him forever.

Jesus had known Father God from the beginning.
Jesus is the only reason this war we're winning.

From Jesus' feet we started learning in the beginning.
There is no other name that can stop us from sinning.

Our stubbornness and pride we must learn to swallow.
Where Jesus leads we must learn to follow.

The trail thru the wilderness, with His blood Jesus clearly marked, He
had paid the cost.
Jesus is waiting for us, He is not willing that any are lost.

JESUS ONLY

Absent from the body present with the Lord.
Jesus paid the price we could not afford.

Jesus is the Way, the Truth, and the Life. There is no other.
If you love Jesus you are His in truth, His sister and brother.

Once we were lost and lonely, no way to turn back.
Then we met Jesus, He put our derailed train on track.

We walk in briers and brambles, our feet don't hurt anymore.
Jesus has taken the hurt out of life; He's the one we walk for.

Jesus holds our heart close to Him, if we love Him only.
If we walk in newness of life, no one will ever again be lonely.

IN JESUS' NAME

The Son of God is the Light of the world all the time man has been
sinning.
The Son has been the Light with the Father from the beginning.

Every knee will bow to Jesus in that hour,
When Jesus stands on the earth in glory and power.

Man without faith is like washing greasy dishes without soap.
Man without God literally hasn't any hope.

Man without God is in a hopeless state.
Man without love is left in the grip of hate.

Man without faith in God is not thankful for life's light.
Without the name of Jesus our days are as night.

In the name of Jesus our enemies will all run.
In the name of Jesus we stand before our enemies as one.

STAND UP FOR JESUS

If we feel the sands of time slipping away,
We have the blessings of Jesus to look forward to everyday.

Those that love God, will have a good attitude.
Those that love God, will be filled with gratitude.

Those that love God, will not try to hide in the night.
Those that love God, will respect God's anointed light.

God calls a few to teach His holy Word.
God calls a few to soar like a bird.

If we are filled with resentment, and know too much pride,
Ask God to forgive you, our sins from God we can't hide.

It is better to be with Jesus, to be known as the least,
Than to have all the world, and draw wages from the beast.

Give it up for Jesus, God knows your heart.
Jesus gave His life; it was God's plan from the start.

Give up what is least; you will gain what is most.
Stand up for Jesus; be healed by God's Holy Ghost.

Calvin Alford

THE UNIVERSE IS OURS

Radiant of the Spirit, glowing with love.
Jesus sent the Comforter, in gentle power like a dove.

Father God wants us to help each other to reach for the stars.
Jesus is willing to give us the universe, if we ask it's already ours.

Without each other we can't enjoy what God gives.
Satan tried to take for himself, now he no longer lives.

God is greater than all of our combined understanding,
If we all work together, victory will be ours with our demanding.

We can't lift others up without becoming closer to heavenly poise,
Helping others grow can be one of life's greatest joys.

The universe is all existing things, earth and its creatures and all
heavenly bodies and things.
All of this is what God promises, that's what God's love brings.

Believe that you have already received the promises of God.
If we trust God we will have a harvest; Jesus has already planted and
turned the sod.

I

See

Jesus

Book Two

JESUS LOVES YOU

Don't be afraid, little ones of the dark night.
Jesus is with you until morning light.

His love surrounds you all through the day,
When you are at school and when you are at play.

There is not a moment that Jesus doesn't see,
The things in your heart and what you can be.

His love surrounds you both night and day.
He hears your prayers and what you pray.

WHAT WILL I DO

When I kneel down by my bed to pray,
Jesus, please hear me, what I have to say.

Jesus, please don't let Mommy and Daddy fight anymore,
For I hear them hollering, through my closed bedroom door.

Jesus, I'm only little, I don't know what to do.
Jesus, you are so big, is anything too hard for you?

Jesus, I know you love them, and I love them, too.
Jesus, if they don't stay together, what will I do?

JESUS WAS SENT

Some men see in others
only evil, and are lonely.
Some believers see in others,
Jesus Christ only.

Some believers look inside themselves,
and strive to improve.
Some men think they are already
right in the grave.

Some men have seen Jesus,
and were born again.
Some men are happy
to remain in their sin.

It is not the healthy that need
a doctor, but the sick.
Believe in Jesus to save
others right quick.

Jesus was sent to give
sight to the blind.
Those that love Jesus
will be loving and kind.

Look beyond what you see
in man with the eye.
And to the world each day,
be sure to die.

JESUS WATCHES OVER YOU

When we have done
everything we possibly can,
Jesus can do what's
impossible for man.

Jesus' disciples gathered
a few loaves of bread;
With only two fish
over 5,000 men Jesus fed.

When Jesus' disciples were straining
at the oars in the black of the night,
Jesus came walking on water,
they were filled with fright.

The disciples thought they were seeing a ghost,
Jesus said, "Don't you know
I'm always watching
over you wherever you go?"

When the disciples were afraid
of the size of the wave,
Jesus was praying to the Father,
their blessing He gave.

If you knew Jesus as well
as He knows you,
God still loves you,
no matter what you do.

If you are frightened,
and don't' know what to do,
Let Jesus come in,
He is very close to you.

JESUS IS THE KING

If you shop in the Devil's storehouse,
the price is always high.
God has good things for you here on earth,
and in the sweet by and by.

If you shop in the Devil's storehouse,
it could cost you an arm and a leg.
God can mend your broken heart,
even though you are sitting on a powder keg.

The Devil breaks everything you touch,
if you're shopping in his store.
Only God has the power to heal,
and make things last forever more.

If you have something broken,
because you were doing your own thing,
Jesus is alive forevermore,
Jesus is the King.

GOD LOVED ME FIRST

When I was young,
I just wanted to have fun.
When I got older,
I met God's son.

He forgave me my sins
on that very day,
Then he began to show me
the most excellent way.

The best things in life
are free, I've been told.
Friends are the best,
if I may be so bold.

Brothers and sisters,
you know God loves you,
God loved me first,
now, I love you too.

LOVE GOD

Don't be afraid to enter the land
flowing with milk and honey.
Wandering in the desert
forty years is not funny.

Cross over the Jordan River
on dry land.
If you are obedient to God,
He will give you a hand.

Hear, O Israel, and be careful to obey,
in keeping God's decrees and commands.
With trembling and fear in God,
you are in His hands.

We cannot make ourselves
one inch taller,
Without God's help we
will become even smaller.

The Lord our God is one
in Jesus Christ, the Son.
With the Holy Spirit
the three of them are one.

If we learn eternal truths in the loving
environment of a God fearing home,
loving God with all ourselves,
our hearts will never roam.

TAX COLLECTORS

I am Matthew,
a Jewish tax collector, you see.
At least I was,
until the man Jesus set me free.

Not an ordinary man
that you might meet.
At my tax booth collecting,
I saw Jesus coming down the street.

My heart leaped into my throat,
as down the street I ran.
Something stirred deep within me;
I had to see this man.

I'm short and could not see Jesus
Amongst all that crowd,
So I climbed up in a tree
and shouted right out loud.

Jesus stopped, looked up at me,
and said, "Come down right away.
I'm going to eat at your house,
on this very day."

Being close to Jesus
has made me feel so alive.
Now I'm here at my house,
I can't wait for Him to arrive.

Although my large house is furnished
with the finest in the land,
It doesn't make me worthy to feel
the touch of the Messiah's hand.

I've invited many people
to meet Jesus face to face.
Now He is really coming,
He is coming to my place.

I know Jesus,
I've seen Him raise the dead.
When He heals the sick,
to Him I bow my head.

Jesus was the Son of David,
but His kingdom is not of this earth.
His kingdom is without end,
and therefore of much greater worth.

(Scripture References: *Luke 5:27-32; 19:1-10)*

THE ONLY WAY

Focus on God's love, not man.
Jesus can save you, only He can.

If you trust in God, blessings will flow.
You will walk in power wherever you go.

Take the hand of Jesus that is offered to you.
You'll feel the power of God in the things you do.

If you want the best for the people you love,
The best is Jesus, the one from above.

Pray that Jesus will hear what we pray,
Jesus, we know you are the only way.

PLEASE FORGIVE ME

Anger in the head is not so bad.
But anger in the heart is really sad.

Anger hurts others but it hurts us, too.
Holding a grudge isn't something we should do.

If we forgive others and turn the other cheek,
It does not mean in any way we are weak.

If we cannot control our anger, we are not strong.
Our downfall is coming, it won't be long.

If your enemy wants your coat, give him your shirt, too.
There is nothing better for me to do.

If you forgive me, Jesus promises to forgive you.
Please understand, it is the right thing to do.

SALVATION

If you have a job, do you get
your wages first of all,
or do you have to build the house
and finish up the wall?

If someone does some work for you,
do you tell them to go away.
or does the law require that you
have to give them pay?

If you go into the grocery store,
get food and walk away,
as you pass the checkout stand,
tell the checker, "Have a nice day."

What do you think would happen,
if your bills you did not pay.
But merely told the phone company,
"Catch me another day."

Now the price of your salvation,
you do not have to pay a thing.
The total price has been paid
by Jesus Christ, the King.

I'VE SEEN JESUS

I've seen Jesus in town today,
As I watched two children play.

I saw Jesus go into the store,
I watched an old man as he held the door.

I saw Jesus in the morning sunrise,
And again I saw Jesus in my wife's eyes.

I saw Jesus as I walked down the road,
This man was helping another with a heavy load.

I saw Jesus go into the school,
As a teacher carried in her heart the, "Golden Rule."

I've seen Jesus all over town today,
So I got on my knees and began to pray.

Jesus, teach me what I need to know,
To follow You everywhere that You go.

THIS WAY TO JESUS

God loves you and you have proof in Jesus, the Son.
Salvation is free for you and me and everyone.

Wait on the Lord, praise God and shout out loud.
And please don't worry if all the noise draws a great crowd.

If you have a little to give in faith and love,
Jesus can increase the little you have up to heaven above.

When it comes time to harvest what has been planted in prayer,
Those that love Jesus will surely be there.

With rolled up sleeves and pointing the way,
This way to Jesus, have a wonderful day.

IT'S TRUE, THE BIBLE

The Bible is the living Word
of God, you can be sure.
If anyone was made by God,
you were.

Only God can make a tree
started from one small seed.
God has all the answers
for anything you need.

If you have any doubt
that the Bible is totally true,
Jesus has a plan that is
written down for you.

Ask God to forgive you,
and take away all your sin.
He can make your life
totally new again.

TRUST JESUS

Jesus wants you to come to Him,
just the way you were.
Jesus is the Son of God,
of this I'm forever sure.

The more convinced we become,
that Jesus is really God's Son,
the mighty works of God's Spirit
show the three of them are one.

Jesus' mighty works of power and love
show us He is able to save one and all.
His miracles of forgiveness bring healing
when we trust in Him like Paul.

YOU ONLY HAVE FOREVER

Take the hand of Jesus
and walk along with Him.
With Jesus you have a future
instead of sink or swim.

When you walk in the light of Jesus,
you won't stumble along the way.
There won't be any darkness,
Jesus' light fills up the day.

When your heart is light and you
are filled with the light of love,
Jesus has sent just what you need
from heaven up above.

Although the path is narrow that
leads to where you want to go,
Jesus can lead you safely, He is
the One you need to know.

When life seems almost over, remember,
in Jesus you have a friend.
You have a new beginning
of a life that will never end.

I VISITED MATTHEW

I went to visit Matthew today,
to listen to what he had to say.

He said Jesus was sent
by God's own hand,
to teach us exactly
what the Father has planned.

He said Jesus taught people
in many ways,
and if we will listen,
there will be no end to our days.

He said Jesus did miracles,
more than a few.
If we listen to Matthew carefully,
we will know what to do.

Matthew saw Jesus as He hung on the cross,
yet he came back to life again.
Jesus did this,
to save us from sin.

Matthew said our job is to tell
Jesus' story to all the earth,
and live what we teach,
for all it is worth.

I VISITED MARK

I went to visit Mark on my walk
through the world today,
And listened very carefully
to what he had to say.

He showed me where Jesus walked
as He taught the Sermon on the Mount,
and where He told the people
to sit here and there all around.

The things that Mark told me,
the things that I heard,
are the things that Jesus said,
His living Word.

Jesus spoke about divorce,
and about the hardness of man's heart;
and about the riches of man
keeping God and man apart.

Mark talked about the Last Supper,
even though he was not there.
Jesus tells us everything,
because He really does care.

The Spirit of God moved rapidly,
towards a climax, it's easy to see.
The crucifixion and the resurrection,
are the way it had to be.

If you don't think God moves rapidly,
when it comes to you and me,
Well, I guess you had to be there,
when Jesus died to set us free.

Now you must move quickly,
don't even try to stall.
There may yet be time to be forgiven,
before Jesus gives that final call.

JOHN THE BAPTIST

In the wilderness John baptized,
when people confessed their sins.
They went under the water in the Jordan River,
John lifted them up again.

John wore clothing made of camel's hair,
with a leather belt around his waist.
He ate locusts and wild honey
with humility and good taste.

John said, "One is coming after me,
more powerful than I.
The thongs of his sandals,
I am not worthy to untie.

"I baptize you with water,
But He will baptize you with the Holy Spirit.
He has the words of salvation,
If you will only hear it."

John said, "I must become less,
and He must become more.
He is the key to heaven
that opens up the door.

THE ANSWER

If you want answers when you pray,
Walk close to Jesus every day.

If you have lots of fences to mend,
Treat Jesus like your best friend.

If you see others that have a need,
Don't let your heart be ruled by greed.

Give to Jesus all the glory.
Then you will know the rest of the story.

You only need to read the end of the book.
The Holy Spirit will give you the answer when you look.

Put a smile on your face.
Take Jesus with you every place.

The answer is right in front of you.
Jesus is the answer, I thought you knew.

ALTHOUGH WE MAY APPEAR

Although we may appear
to be at the end of our rope,
In Jesus, there is
no end to our hope.

Although it may appear
that we haven't got a prayer,
There is nothing to worry about
because Jesus is there.

Although we appear
to be standing alone in the dark,
Jesus is with us,
it's a walk in the park.

We can have victory,
day after day,
If we trust in Jesus
to carry us all the way.

If we keep the promise
of God in our heart,
the things of the world
won't be able to tear us apart

If you have a problem
that is too big for you,
give it to Jesus,
He knows what to do.

GOD'S TRUTH

The one that has God's truth
will walk in power.
All day long, hour after hour.

The one that has God's truth
will bless others.
Fathers, mothers, sisters, brothers.

The one that has God's truth
will give to all.
He heard Jesus when He gave the call.

The one that has God's truth
will seek God night and day,
Because he knows there is no other way.

GOD IS ALWAYS THERE

When you plant seed,
plant as much as you can.
For the hand of God
is not limited by man.

Give freely to those
that have the need.
God will plant with you,
He will increase your seed.

Have faith in God,
He's where miracles come from.
Ask God for miracles,
He will give you some.

God said, "My house
is a house of prayer."
If we go to God's house,
He is always there.

If we plant seed,
and ask God to make it grow,
He will give the increase,
His Word says so.

THE GREATEST COMMANDMENT

Love the Lord your God with all your heart.
If you do this you have a good start.

Love the Lord your God with all your soul,
And the devil's arrows will not take their toll.

Love the Lord your God with all your mind,
And to your neighbor be loving and kind.

Yet there is one more thing you should do.
Don't forget to be loving and kind to you.

THE HEART WITHIN

Jesus doesn't look at the height of man,
or the color of his skin.
Jesus looks beyond all that to the heart
that is within.

Jesus said if we center our life on the things
of this earth,
We will miss all the things that are of
much greater worth.

If we give up our self-centered determination
to be in charge,
Our treasure in heaven will be
twice as large.

Follow Jesus, miss all things
in hell.
Spend an eternity in heaven
as well.

INCREASING FAITH

True obedience comes from the heart.
If we love Jesus, the devil has no part.

Live for Christ, even when no one is looking to see.
More like Christ is what we want to be.

Trying to live by the law of flesh given by man,
Is impossible to do, no one can.

God is spirit and must be worshipped in spirit.
If you pray in the flesh, God won't hear it.

Pray in the spirit without ceasing,
With faith in God ever increasing.

JESUS IS KNOCKING

Sorry, Jesus, I don't have time today,
to read your word or stop to pray.

Sorry, Jesus, I don't have time right now,
Maybe another time I will have time to plow.

That seed that you wanted me to plant yesterday;
there was a game of golf I had to play.

I'm sorry, Jesus, that fence you wanted me to mend;
on that day I had to go sailing with a friend.

I'm so busy I don't have time anymore,
to answer Jesus as He knocks at the door.

JESUS IS THE WAY

There is a message,
that you need to hear.
Listen to Jesus,
He will make everything clear.

He wants to tell you
He's always loved you,
He will forgive you
in all that you do.

He has been waiting
all of your life long.
When you are weak in your life,
He is strong.

Stand on the promise
that He's given to you.
Jesus wants to heal
and make you brand new.

Jesus is waiting,
He is waiting for you today.
Come home to Jesus,
for He is the way.

JESUS FOREVER

Jesus can be seen
everywhere you look.
Down at the soup kitchen,
I have seen the cook.

The cook had a smile
on his face,
While thinking of Jesus
he'd seen in that place.

Jesus came to town
to set everyone free.
I see Jesus praying
for you and me.

When Jesus prays he takes requests
from those that care.
Jesus spreads love and hope,
and treats everyone fair.

Please don't worry,
everything is okay.
Believe in Jesus,
He is here to stay.

REVELATION

No matter what happens,
Revelation shows that God is in control.
So, look here, let's all be ready,
when Jesus calls the roll.

Drink deeply of the living water
that is told of in the Word,
for many people are dying,
at least that's what I've heard.

Water of life is free,
it cannot be earned.
Look to Jesus for the answer,
and keep from being burned.

If you are dying of thirst,
I cannot make you drink.
It's my hope as you read this poem,
that I can make you think.

You crossed paths with Jesus,
yet you looked the other way.
Soon, you will have to face Him,
when it comes to Judgment Day.

Jesus is waiting,
on the first road that you took.
Now He is in Revelation,
on every page you look.

JESUS GIVES

Jesus said pray for yourselves,
when facing the darkest hour.
He died for us and rose again,
like the dew that's on the flower.

Jesus rose and went on ahead,
to prepare a place for us to be.
Mansions beyond compare, shimmering
like the sun shining on the sea.

There is no darkness
where Jesus is at.
Please get in the boat,
you can see where Jesus sat.

Jesus wants us to stay busy
for our neighbor's sake.
We will see Jesus in the least of these,
when we give instead of take.

When Jesus is in the boat with us,
the trip is never long.
When we are weak and weary,
in us Jesus is strong.

The Good

Shepherd

Book Three

CHOSEN OF GOD

We have been chosen of God when we asked
and He forgave us all our sin.
We have been chosen of God
when we gave up our old life and begin to live again.

We have been chosen of God
when we become tired of being lost;
When we see the hate
and tally up the cost.

We have been chosen of God when we forgive others
in spite of the pain and lack of trust.
Please don't hang onto pain
just because you feel you must.

We have been chosen of God
when we choose to come to Him in love.
All the anger gone away
as gentle as a dove.

It's your choice to love
or hold onto hate.
You must make the choice
in your hands lies your fate.

(**Scripture Reference:** *Ephesians 2:8*)

IN THE LORD'S HANDS

Fear the Lord and gain peace for your heart and soul.
To know Jesus should be every man's goal.

When the light breaks in on man's understanding,
He will no longer give into the devil's demands.

Remain in the Lord's hands and He will mold you
to be like Him only.
If you do your own thing you will continue to be lonely.

There is a way that seems right to man.
Run away from that to God as fast as you can.

THE LIGHT IS JESUS

God sees all your tears and feels the pain you have for others.
As you walk along the narrow path of life leaving behind
sisters and brothers.

God watches over you as you try to show the way.
God is drawing you closer to Him in love
saying child it is okay.

God is building in you eternity that no man can take away.
Pray the light will shine bright in us until that last day.

You have heard of the light at the end of the tunnel,
it could be an oncoming train.
The light I see is Jesus; He will take away the pain.

JESUS IS ALL

Let's all put on a smile.
Are you ready to walk a mile for Jesus?

Let's all make friends.
Are you ready to make amends for Jesus?

Let's all help to make someone laugh.
Are you ready to cut you loneliness in half for Jesus?

Do you have life all planed out?
Or, is it time to give a shout for Jesus?

Are you going to take a break?
Or, are you going to walk across the lake for Jesus?

Are you going to sit in the park?
Or, are you going to build an ark for Jesus?

Are you going to procrastinate?
Or, are you going to stop the hate for Jesus?

Are you going to do just a little?
Or, are you going to get right in the middle for Jesus?

Are you sitting home getting bored?
Or, are you waiting on the Lord?
That's Jesus.

WALK WITH JESUS

Walk with Jesus from the start.
He will fix the ache that is in your heart.

Walk with Jesus, let Him lead.
He is the one that knows our need.

Let your love in Christ run very deep.
Don't give up the things God wants you to keep.

Don't be fooled, don't be deceived.
Hang onto what Christ first taught and you first believed.

Take Jesus with you everywhere you go.
You can be certain you will reap the kind of seed you sow.

If you tell someone the truth for their own good,
make sure you first are doing the things you should.

CHANGE

Change yourself first it will encourage all the rest,
if you want others to change for the best.

Go to a higher level of caring in the things that you do,
if you want the other guy to be more like you.

First pull the plank from your own eye my brother,
if you would remove the speck from the eye of another.

Seek first God He has a few hills for you to climb,
if you would change the world one person at a time.

Lift your eyes up, no don't look at me,
if you want others to be the best that they can be.

Learn to love others and get a free sample.
Jesus is our perfect example.

I BELIEVE

Although I appear to have failed in the things I have done
from day to day,
Jesus tells me He still loves me, so I can't be a failure,
there isn't any way.

It isn't good to look back,
if Lot were here he would tell you so.
As you travel along the road of life,
look ahead there is a bright future for the ones that know.

If you look in the mirror and see one
that hasn't got a friend,
Help your neighbor to see the rainbow,
the pot of gold is at the other end.

I believe in miracles,
in my life I have seen a few.
Jesus has a bunch of miracles,
He is saving just for you.

The more important question is not "to be,
or not to be."
The way I see it, the question is,
has Jesus set you free.

(Scriptural References: *Acts 15:12; John 2:11; Matthew 12:28*)

PURE GOLD

Our God wants to make of us
the likeness of pure gold.
Our God wants us to live forever
with His love we can't grow old.

74

Our God wants to mold and shape us
to the likeness of pure gold.
Jesus has purchased us
to fit into His custom designed mold.

Bow down and draw close to Jesus
He wants to fix your heart.
When our hearts become broken
then the healing can start.

So you say that there are too many things in your life
that can't be fixed.
Jesus has a special medicine
just for you that He has mixed.

Do you want to be like Jesus
then you have to fit the mold.
We have to get out the impurity in us
because Jesus is pure gold.

PLANTING SEED

Planting seed in the right place,
can put smiles on many a face.

Planting seeds of love where only weeds have grown,
can produce a beautiful garden, this fact is known.

When you plant a garden with seeds that are good,
don't forget to ask God for help, I wish you would.

When we plant seeds it's best to plant a lot.
When it comes to harvest time, give to those who have not.

When a garden is planted with giving to others in mind,
when harvest time comes, it will give sight to the blind.

OUR REDEEMER

God is right even if man is not.
Man doesn't do what he is taught.

If we don't do what we know is the right thing to do,
We can't teach our children to pray all the way through.

We teach by example, our children drink the water from our well.
Are we teaching our children the way to hell?

We do have a redeemer that teaches what is right.
If we learn from Jesus, we will win the fight.

We can only teach what we have learned.
If we learn from Satan we need to be concerned.

Jesus is the redeemer of mankind.

(**Scriptural References:** *Matthew 12:29-30; Revelation 20:10*)
(Refer to **reference 1,** pg. 150 in the section of **Personal Notations and Thoughts** on righteousness and temptation.)

FATHER OF AGES

I've seen this very old couple walking down the street,
the woman was very lovely her white hair glistened in the sun.
The two of them walking together,
they seemed to be as one.

They seemed to be praying,
as some hoodlums came their way.
The old man tried to straighten up and smiled,
he said, "Boys have a nice day."

The leader of the pack in an angry voice said,
"Get out of my way."
As he kicked the cane from the old man's hand,
and looked down at where he lay.

The old man looked up at him
with a smile still on his face.
"There isn't anything you can to do me
my home is in another place."

The young man said with a sneer,
"I know where you live I recognize your face.
And, now that you have offended me,
I'm coming by your place."

The old man said, "I will be ready.
I have a special friend, I want you to meet.
When I first met this friend,
He made my life complete."

The old woman helped her husband
to stand on his feet.
She said to the young man,
"Bring your friends you will be surprised at who you will meet."

(Refer to **reference 2** on pg. 150 in the section of **Personal Notations and Thoughts** on friendship.)

FOREVER

When Lot left Sodom and Gomorrah,
he didn't take a thing.
He took only His trust in God,
knowing the trouble the rest would bring.

Lot walked away not looking back
to see the fate of the others.
His daughters watched in shock when they saw
the fate of their mother.

Not knowing what to do,
Lot took a drink to ease the pain.
God had to stop Sodom and Gomorrah,
their world had gone insane.

The world has gone beyond all that,
it's time to believe now or never.
Thank God for believers,
our happy ending will last forever.

Abraham chose to follow God,
Lot was pulled aside by greed.
If we tend to the needs of others,
God will give us all we need.

(**Scriptural Reference:** *Genesis 19*)

THE HAND OF JESUS

The more you love Jesus the more God leads you.
The more you love others, God knows your heart too.

God has a seal that He has put on you and me.
There isn't anything you do that God doesn't see.

Trust in Jesus with the little you have.
He gives us the increase, like miracle healing salve.

If you feel small take the hand of Jesus, it is bigger than life today.
You can give the hand of Jesus to others He will show them the way.

If others are having a struggle and don't know what to do,
Give them the hand of Jesus, that Jesus first gave to you.

Jesus planted seed into man 2,000 years ago.
We are the harvest planted by Jesus in love you know.

The hand of Jesus does not belong to only a few.
Jesus' hand is big enough to cover sin in all we do.

(**Scriptural Reference:** *1 Corinthians 4:5*)

LOVE NEVER ENDS

Love seeks not its own.
The love of Christ Jesus by many is known.

Love seeks not its own.
If you love Christ Jesus you are not alone.

Love seeks what it can give.
God wants us all to live.

Love is patient and kind.
It looks for the good that it can find.

Love does not insist on its own way.
It seeks the good of others when we pray.

Love does not rejoice at wrong but rejoices in the right.
When love sees injustice it will fight.

The things of this earth will pass away some day.
But when perfection comes, the imperfect will pass away.

When love fights hate, let me say it again.
When love fights hate, in the end love will win.

(**Scriptural Reference:** *1 Corinthians 13:1-13*)
(Refer to **reference 3** on pg. 150 in the section of **Personal Notations and Thoughts** on real, lasting love.)

SOWING SEED

America is sowing seed into the lives of others.
God is increasing His love in the lives of our brothers.

America is lovely when in it God's increasing love is seen.
Life is in the blood of our Savior who in every way cleans.

God create in us a clean heart to pray for each other.
So we can walk beside not on top of our brother.

Plan to love deeply for the day is near.
God's purpose and plan is increasingly clear.

Pay every debt that is in God's Word.
Don't ever stop loving the truth that you have heard.

Let's step out of the darkness and step into the light.
When the storm is over the dawn replaces the night.

LOVE IS STRONGER

Jesus loves you Bin Laden, but no one loves the things you do.
Jesus loves you Bin Laden, but you bite the hand that feeds you.

Jesus loves you Bin Laden, but you will reap the things you sow.
Jesus loves you Bin Laden, He is the one you need to know.

Jesus loves you Bin Laden, the things you love will not save you.
Jesus loves you Bin Laden, some people may go to hell
before you're through.

Friends don't let Bin Laden infect you with what's in his heart.
Love is stronger than the hate that keeps tearing this world apart.

(**Scriptural Reference:** *Jeremiah 2:17-20*)
(Refer to **reference 4** on pg. 150 in the section of **Personal Notations and Thoughts** about Jesus' far reaching love.)

I BELONG TO JESUS

I belong to Jesus because He found me naked and in shame.
I had no more hope left; I am so very glad He came.

I was in darkness and the cold hung all around me, night without day.
I've seen the light of Jesus and felt the warmth come in to stay.

All the time I was frightened, nowhere to turn and hide.
If only I could find a friend, I was full of earthly pride.

When no one else wanted me because I was such a mess
and all alone.
Jesus said, "Come to my warmth and light and fellowship
around my throne.

BE SURE

The wrath of God is coming on the people of the earth.
Thank God for Jesus and His plan of new birth.

If you have fear of the things that are coming upon man,
Run hide in the arms of Jesus to save you is His plan.

You ask me how I know these things, how can I be sure.
I read it in the Word of God, all the answers there they were.

Yes I have joy, I know I'm completely safe, Jesus is my Rock.
I'm under the master's protection, now it's time to do the walk.

It's time to pray the prayer of faith for others.
If we pray all the way thru on the other side we are all brothers.

GOD SAID NO

God don't want us to be blind, He wants us to see.
God don't want us to be bound, God wants us to be free.

God wants us to have faith, God will make the walls fall down.
God wants us to walk after Jesus; He is worthy to wear the crown.

God wants us to understand so He repeats what He wants us to hear.
God is telling us eternal things, for our sake He wants to make things clear.

If we would have listened the first time when God told us no,
When man was in the garden perhaps we might not have had to go.

GOD'S GRACE

Jesus died to give us a chance to live again.
God's grace is greater than all our sin.

The things of this world they will not last.
The blood of Jesus sweeps away all of our past.

The things of this world will pass away.
We will all stand before God on judgment day.

All eyes will see Jesus come down again.
To put an end to what was started by sin.

God will make you more than you dreamed you could be.
He will prepare you to walk in love and humility.

When the snow covers the ground you can't see the dirt.
When God's grace covers our sin we can't see the hurt.

God help us to be prepared to know where to start.
God will give us the desires of our heart.

WORKING IN LOVE

Jesus said I have food to eat that you know nothing of;
To do the work of my Father in heavenly love.

The fields are ripe, the harvest of enormous size.
Jesus told His disciples to open their eyes.

The fields are being harvested as we speak.
Jesus is with us, the Savior we seek.

God gives the increase and all things are new.
We are all reaping benefits of the work of a few.

One gives away and another keeps.
One sows and another reaps.

If we don't open our eyes, at the judgment we will grieve.
Unless some see miracles they will not believe.

We are standing closer to the kingdom each day.
If we follow Jesus He is showing us the way.

(**Scriptural Reference:** *John 4:32-38*)
(Refer to **reference 5** on pg. 150 in the section of **Personal Notations and Thoughts** on the Lord's will.)

FOREVER LOVE

Jesus is the Vine and we are the branches.
If we bear good fruit, we have more advances.

God trims and prunes all the dead wood away,
If we follow Jesus in love when we pray.

If we follow Jesus and bear much fruit in love,
God will multiply your treasure in heaven above.

You are clean because Jesus' words in your heart were hidden deep.
Pray without ceasing, remain in Jesus, do not love sleep.

Ask for what you want, it will be given to you.
Don't turn from Jesus in the things you do.

Your joy will be complete if you love each other.
God's kind of love is for you and me brother.

Jesus in love will call us sister and brother,
When we remain in love for each other.

We are Jesus' friend if we do what He asks.
His love is forever that's how long it lasts.

(Scriptural Reference: *John 15:1-17)*

THE NARROW DOOR

Many will look for God in all the wrong places.
Searching for God with pride in their faces.

Without any help then we will burn in the fire.
Searching for love without looking higher.

To get through the narrow door, we will have to work together.
Help each other to get through stormy weather.

If we don't help others to open the narrow door,
Jesus will say I don't know you anymore.

If we say Jesus I really know you,
And yet, did we become too busy in the things we do?

Jesus taught the way through the narrow door.
If we do likewise, we will live forever more.

We were all warned so now guess what?
The time will come when the door will be shut.

Jesus wants to call us all His brother, sister, and mother.
Be kind and loving to one another.

(**Scriptural Reference:** *Luke 13:22-30*)

PRISON

We are in prison we have made for self.
When we fail to pick up our Bible lying in the dust on the shelf.

We are in prison with the walls stretching way up high.
We can break out of prison if only we will try.

There is no need to be all alone in a dark cold cell.
God is not willing that we should go to hell.

Don't struggle and fight to be free all alone.
Jesus can take away your chains you can walk out on your own.

We need Jesus to guide us along the narrow way.
Jesus will stay beside us when we kneel to pray.

Within we have a prison that only God can see.
Jesus says you can be anything that you want to be.

OUR NEIGHBOR
IS A KEEPER

Only if you have the anointing of God can you see men healed.
With the power of God our salvation is sealed.

With trust and faith in God and our knee bent in prayer,
The God that loves us will always be there.

As we believe God will provide everything that our neighbor needs,
God still wants us to give from our heart and plant some seeds.

When we rise up in the dawn to start a new day,
The opportunities unfold when we kneel down to pray.

When we look at our neighbors' fields and we see them full of weeds,
The good things that God has given us is what our neighbor needs.

NO MORE FEAR

Jesus came to separate us from the guilt of our sin,
To give us the choice to choose life once again.

Jesus did not leave us with no way to win,
He sent us a comforter to bring life within.

There is no need to complain or to pout,
He gave us a plan, in the Bible it's laid out.

A shout for Jesus, He is the only way.
Take Jesus with you to be saved every day.

Jesus is the king that we can trust.
He leaves our tears behind in the dust.

(**Scriptural Reference:** *1 Corinthians 10:24*)
(Refer to **reference 6** on pg. 150 in the section of **Personal Notations and Thoughts** on what it means to be saved.)

THE ANSWER

Waiting on man can be to no avail,
Like waiting for the ship to come in that has no sail.

This can leave you cold instead of warm.
Waiting for the dawn to arrive after the storm.

Life can be hard, from beginning to end.
Waiting for boys to grow into men.

We will cover sin and avoid much grief and pain,
If we help others to grow in love and peace, we will gain.

Waiting for winter to turn into spring,
When it arrives can make your heart sing.

There is an answer to all of the above.
Follow Jesus in God's kind of love.

(**Scriptural Reference:** *Exodus 20:20*)
(Refer to **reference 7** on pg. 150 in the section of **Personal Notations and Thoughts** love and fear.)

SIX THOUSAND YEARS

Even though my eyes are filled with tears,
Jesus said the things I say you don't want to hear.

It all started with a single lie.
Satan said, "Eat the fruit, you will not die."

Eve said to Adam, "Come, eat of the fruit of the tree.
Your eyes will be open and you will see."

Adam said, "What? Okay dear."

Stop and think what you are about to say.
Don't let the sun set on your anger at the end of the day.

After the lie and the hurt come the tears.
And that's the way it's been for six thousand years.

What I mean brothers and sisters is this.
We can betray Jesus with only one kiss.

(**Scriptural References:** *1 Corinthians 1:18-2:16; 11:23-29; 13:1-13; 15:42-58*)
(Refer to **reference 8** on pg. 151 in the section of **Personal Notations and Thoughts** on blessings and eternity.)

Rejoice

in the

LORD!

Book

four

THE GOLDEN RULE

Satan bites man like the poison of a snake.
Sin invades our life with a lure like a beautiful cake.

Sin starts from within our own hearts.
That's where the beginning of trouble starts.

Contentment with godliness is of great gain.
When covetousness flows through our life,
it's poison in our veins.

Satan hurts the ones he can fool.
Stay close to Jesus, remember the golden rule.

The life and times of man are short, the game of life's story.
Be sure to learn and practice each day, be it all to God's glory.

(Scriptural Reference: Matthew 7:7-12)

PREACH AND PRACTICE

Lots of people know how to preach,
But few of them know how to practice.

Lots of people know how to correct others,
Very few listen to their fathers and mothers.

Lots of children know all things?
How many parents give children the peace that love brings?

Lots of people like to be called brothers.
Only a few have respect for their fathers and mothers.

Lots of people know Jesus died for our sins.
How many know Jesus is where life begins?

(Scriptural References: Joshua 5:13-15; 6:1-17)
(Refer to **reference 9** on pg. 151 in the section of **Personal Notations and Thoughts** on victory.)

TIME IS SHORT

When it comes to love, do you count the cost?
Jesus went to Calvary and gave His life
to regain what man had lost.

Of those that love Jesus, He hasn't lost any.
Of those that believe and trust Jesus from one to many.

God's love does not only include this group of people here
or that one there.
The salvation from God is offered to all of us everywhere.

If we have no fire in us, we can't start a fire.
It helps to come to practice if we want to sing in the Church choir.

Satan's time is short, that's the way I believe and feel.
The judgment of God will be Satan's last meal.

(Scriptural References: Hebrews 10:24, 25)

A NEW DAY RISING

Jesus is the all-time best, you see.
A life saving time of opportunity.

You can get in right now, on the ground floor.
Hurry before the Bridegroom shuts the door.

You can learn the business before it's too late.
One thing though, you will have to surrender all your hate.

The opportunities to grow are virtually unlimited, at this time.
The benefits to be saved are out of this world, up the ladder
you will climb.

In this opportunity there is only one way that's up, all the way.
Jesus is coming back soon, only God knows the day.

There is a new day rising, it's on its way.
Do you know the cost Jesus has had to pay?

The world is spinning out of control with hate.
The only thing that can stop it is love, God holds our fate.

(Scriptural References: Matthew 3:8; 25:1-13; Acts 13:50)
(Refer to **reference 10** on pg. 151 in the section of **Personal Notations and Thoughts** on changed life.)

LOVE AND GLORY

Today is the day that God has made.
Lift up your eyes and be unafraid.

Go forth in love standing straight and tall.
No need to hide, no none at all.

If we walk with Jesus we will know the whole story.
We will sing praise to God from here to glory.

You can't match a vulture to a gentle dove.
You can't start with hate to build on love.

(Scriptural References: Matthew 22:37-40; Luke 7:30; 10:25; 11:45; 14:3)
(Refer to **reference 11** on pg. 151 in the section of **Personal Notations and Thoughts** on loving God and others.)

SOLD OUT TO JESUS

Sold out to Jesus, He has paid full price for me.
Although I felt worthless before Jesus set me free.

Sold out to Jesus, without Him for me there was no more hope.
My life I had wasted, I felt just like a dope.

Sold out to Jesus, I wandered about.
In total confusion, my life running out.

Sold out to Jesus, I was drowning in sin.
Jesus has saved me, I'm living again.

(Scriptural References: John 1:29-34; 2 Corinthians 5:21)
(Refer to **reference 12** on pg. 151 in the section of **Personal Notations and Thoughts** on the great exchange.)

LOVE HEALS

When I was a child, when my dad was about to correct me,
He would say, "Son this is going to hurt me more than it'll hurt you.

When He was thru with me I said to myself, "That really hurt.
I think you're wrong Dad."
Not long ago Jesus said to me, 'It has hurt me more than it hurt you.'"

Now I am beginning to understand.
When I was a child I sometimes preferred to stand up
when I ate supper.

Now I give more thought to Jesus' last supper.

Our Father God loves us too much to leave us the way we are.

Any trial we go thru, we can be sure that Jesus is right there
with us, if we let Him be.

It's past time to stop the hurt for Jesus. Hate hurts, love heals.

There is no doubt our Savior knows how hate feels.

LOVE'S NOT FORGOTTEN

Love, love even though hate doesn't love love.
Jesus was here when Satan fell from above.

God loves to see us be kind to each other.
Hate doesn't even like its own brother.

Hate has only itself to please.
Love forgives the mistakes it sees.

Hate is lost, even before it begins.
Love goes on to forgive repentant sins.
Hate doesn't want to see us free; it's not even our friend.
Love is the best of things in us, from beginning to end.

Hate feeds on the suffering; it can cause people to be blind.
Love feeds the hungry, takes the darkness out of our mind.

Love is all that our heart desires.
Love fills our hearts with life producing fires.

Hate is offended by what it knows.
Love builds up, and then it grows.

Love belongs to us if we give it away.
Hate will be forgotten when love comes to stay.

Hate only loves the things that are rotten.
Hate only wins when love is forgotten.

THE MAP

Have you held a sleeping child, when in a comfortable chair
you sat?
If you are looking for Jesus, I know just where He is at.

Have you ever seen the sunrise after a storm,
when you were all alone at night?
Jesus stills the child in me, turns my darkness into light.

When the storms of adversity threaten to steal away your calm,
Put your trust in Jesus, open your Bible and turn to Psalms.

I know because of what I have seen God do.
The Holy Spirit lives in me, and I am praying that He lives in you.

My God fills the universe in a never ending day.
The mapped out route to heaven, is the Bible, all the way.

(Scriptural References: Romans 1:20; Psalm 119:105)
(Refer to **reference 13** on pg. 152 in the section of **Personal Notations and Thoughts** on God's majesty and revelation.)

PRAYER

The pain of discipline, or the pain of regret,
It's our choice as to what we get.

To serve the Lord is a joy to the heart.
To serve the devil keeps love and us apart.

The winds they blow, the rains come down.
If we send up prayer, it will put stars in our crown.

To be alone with God in fervent prayer,
Jesus prayed all night, the power was there.

Jesus walked on water, gave sight to the blind.
If we ask in faith, God will renew our mind.

(Scriptural Reference: James 5:16-18)
(Refer to **reference 14** on pg. 152 in the section of **Personal Notations and Thoughts** on prayer and communion.)

IT'S TIME

Does not the Bible say don't be a borrower or a lender?
When we belong to God we see His glory and His splendor.

If you borrow from the devil, with your life you may have to pay.
God has great things of much worth to give away.

God gives good things, the devil takes away.
Do we want to live forever, or less than one day?

With God one day is as a thousand years,
a thousand years as one day?
Do we want to complain all our lives or get on our knees
and pray?

The flesh cannot please God; it's in total rebellion all day
and night long.
Ask for the Spirit, tell Jesus you love Him, sing Jesus a song.

God made time, now it seems we don't have time for God.
If you stop and think about it, doesn't that seem a little odd?

If Adam and Eve had stuck with God, when they were still
in the garden,
I'm wondering would God have given them a full pardon?

It really does not matter now after 6,000 years have passed.
What matters now is man going to make the right choice at last?

As for me, Satan is getting a little old.
My treasure is in heaven, I'm grabbing for the gold.

(Scriptural References: Genesis 6:3; 2 Peter 3:8-9)
(Refer to **reference 15** pg. 152 in the section of **Personal Notations and Thoughts** on time running out.)

WE HAVE A MANSION

Once I felt empty, I felt no pride in myself.
When Jesus found me I put my false pride on the shelf.

When Jesus found me I was truly lost and sinking lower each day.
Jesus reached out and grabbed me, now I'm up and on my way.

When I was lost before Jesus found me, I had no tools to build.
Now I have a mansion, every need my Lord has filled.

Once I was desperate, just to see a friendly face.
Now that Jesus has given me life, I'm out to win the race.

I'm ready to climb that mountain, or cross the great divide.
I'm just so very happy, I no longer want to hide.

(Scriptural Reference: John 14:1-3)
(Refer to **reference 16** on pg. 153 in the section of **Personal Notations and Thoughts** on the mansion being prepared for us.)

SON OF MAN

The end of time is almost here.
Let us walk in the light and have no fear.

Things are going along according to plan.
Stay close to Jesus; He is the Savior of man.

When time is over in the garden of strife,
If we belong to Jesus, it's the beginning of life.

Can we pick the kind of life we would live on earth?
Would we choose the path that's of much greater worth?

The way of life is written if we care to look.
Life eternal is guaranteed, in God's holy Book.

Thank God He chose us to be in His plan.
This is only the beginning of life with Jesus, the Son of Man.

(Scriptural Reference: Matthew 24:37-44; 25:1)
(Refer to **reference 17** on pg. 153 in the section of **Personal Notations and Thoughts** about the great wedding yet to come.)

GIFT OF GOD

The Father, Jesus, the Holy Spirit are one.
Remember Jesus and what He has done.

Hold in your heart what Jesus did for us in love.
He left us the promise of eternity, as He rose up above.

Jesus did not sin or tell a lie, He did everything for us you see.
Jesus wants to give us the universe, to give ourselves to God,
is the best we can be.

Jesus is far above all the mountains and barriers that we can see.
Jesus wants us to come to Him; He has the greatest of gifts
for you and me.

Jesus is the gift that God gave to us all.
Jesus is the greatest, no one even comes close, or stands
anywhere near as tall.

(Scriptural Reference: Ephesians 2:8)
(Refer to **reference 18** on pg. 153 in the section of **Personal Notations and Thoughts** about the gift of God.)

LIVING WATER

If you get burned put living water on the fire.
If you get burned, forgive, lift others higher.

If you are looking for forgiveness, the living Word says, "Forgive."
If you need to get a life, teach others how to live.

If you see someone looking for the answer to life's eternal joy,
Introduce them to Jesus; He had to be about the Father's work,
even when He was a boy.

If you long for more than the things you have in this world today,
Give your heart to Jesus, remember others when you pray.

(Scriptural Reference: John 7:38)
(Refer to **reference 19** on pg. 153 in the section of **Personal Notations and Thoughts** about the Living Water.)

BODYGUARD

Jesus is our bodyguard His banner over us is love.
Jesus has forgiven us per our heavenly Father up above.

Jesus walked on ahead of us; He was the first to make the trip.
Because our God is a jealous God Satan better give no lip.

The little girl was sleeping in the arms of Father God fast asleep,
Attended by the Son of Man, Jesus said, "Get up, you have blessings now to reap."

The woman had been placed in the upper room, she was much loved,
Her friends couldn't bear to let her go.
Faith in God lifted her up, the power of God began to flow.

If you don't like the way you were born, try being born again.
God is waiting for you to ask, to lift you out of sin.

(Scriptural References: Leviticus 22:19-21;Song of Solomon 2:4; Luke 8:51-56; Acts 9:36-42; John 3:3,5)
(Refer to **reference 20** on pg. 154 in the section of **Personal Notations and Thoughts** on the Old Testament foreshadow of God's great sacrifice of His Son.)

THE BRIGHT
AND MORNING STAR

Jesus the Christ the Morning Star, He is the one.
Awake in the morning to God's only Son.

From the beginning of time, to this present day,
Jesus was chosen by the Father, He is the way.

Content and happy, no more reason to roam.
One day at a time, we will follow Jesus, all the way home.

Once more we thank You for showing us the way.
The truth is our Savior, the dawn of our life this day.

Jesus our Savior, for all time, is truly our friend.
Our life is only beginning, our days without end.

(Scriptural Reference: Revelation 22:16)
(Refer to **reference 21** on pg. 154 in the section of **Personal Notations and Thoughts** about Jesus Christ as the Bright and Morning Star that must dawn in our souls.)

MY LORD

We live for Jesus, He is our Lord.
We do not lead Jesus; that we could not afford.

He commands our heart, in awe and wonder, not making
a sound at best.
We follow Jesus; He leads us through green pastures,
and tells us to lie down and rest.

Jesus is spirit; He walks thru life with us, if we love Him
all the way.
As our prayers and thoughts go to Him, His cover over us
will stay.

The covering of the Lord is awesome yes indeed.
The covering of the Lord holds everything we need.

*(**Scriptural References:** In regard to the Word of Wisdom—1 Corinthians 12; Ephesians 4; Romans 12)*

THE CROSS

The things Satan has done would make most men sick.
Not to worry, Satan has been beaten with his own stick.

The cross or the stick if you will,
Jesus has climbed that mountain like it was a little mole hill.

I am not saying what Jesus did was easy, I know it was hard.
Just thinking about what Jesus did is enough to make me tired.

His disciples slept when Jesus prayed.
The truth of the matter, they were afraid.

They didn't understand till Jesus arose,
And He was standing before them in pure white clothes.

*(**Scriptural Reference:** Luke 14:25-33)*
(Refer to **reference 22** on pg. 154 in the section of **Personal Notations and Thoughts** on being a disciple of Jesus.)

ONE IN JESUS

I've had a dream from the time I was young,
To know what it is all about, I heard about Jesus in songs that
were sung.

My Jesus owns the cattle on a thousand hills.
If we belong to Jesus, His love will cure our ills.

If we give our heart to Jesus, there will be no more need
for the sun.
The light shining brightly from Jesus will make us all one.

When we get free from the world, and go to Jesus, His glory
sets us free.
Now we are in the hands of Jesus, what a great place to be.

(Scriptural Reference: 1 John 1:5-9)

HOME LIGHT

Lost deep in the wilderness, I was searching for home light.
Then Jesus found me and put an end to my night.

The cold no longer chills me clear to the bone.
God's light surrounds me, with the warmth, I'm no longer alone.

Once I could not see, I chose darkness instead.
Now that I've found Jesus, I'm wondering back then, what was
wrong with my head?

Once I had enemies that stretched around the earth,
Then I chose to be a friend, now I know I have worth.

Some things I don't like to talk about, but Jesus I do.
There is no one but Jesus, you know that is true.

(Scriptural References: Psalm 27:1; Revelation 21:22, 23)

ONE OF A KIND

Gathered together in love, at least two or three.
One in Christ, is what we need to be.

Where two are gathered together in love of one heart and mind,
With faith in God not two but one of a kind.
By God's power it's true.

When it's all said and done, only God knew.
Christians are one of a kind, by God's power it's true.

If we follow Christ, in a loving way, to the end of the road,
We can go the extra mile; help each other to a lighter load.

Only God knows what this all means to man.
Walking close to Jesus, giving each other a hand.

Only God is good in every way, that's what matters to man.
Nothing new under the sun, God has the plan.

(Scriptural Reference: Ephesians 4:11, 12)
(Refer to **reference 23** on pg. 154 in the section of **Personal Notations and Thoughts** on discovering our place in the body of Christ.)

TREE OF LIFE

Many trees in the forest, give strength against the storm
and the wind.
Many people of one heart and mind, when they have been
forgiven it's as if they had not sinned.

God does the forgiving, when each one of us has asked.
When God has forgiven, there is no memory of the past.

The past faded into the darkness destroyed by love.
The song in our hearts, is by the grace of the Father above.

If you give love away, it will not return void, nor will it be lost.
Cast your bread on the water, it will return when on the
waves it's been tossed.

The tree of life in the midst of the Paradise of God's garden,
To Him who overcomes, He will receive a full pardon.

(Scriptural References: Genesis 2:9; Ecclesiastes 11:1; Revelation 22:2)
(Refer to **reference 24** on pg. 155 in the section of **Personal Notations and Thoughts** on the healing that will await us in the new heaven and earth.)

NEW DAY

Jesus came to replace the things of the flesh with the
things of the Spirit.
Listen to Jesus, are you ready to hear it.

Jesus came to give Himself for us, without cost.
We have been redeemed, no longer to be lost.

Jesus paid full price, our guilt we no longer own.
Jesus now lives in us; He will no longer leave us alone.

Jesus bought all the pity, pain, and hate.
It's time to go on with Jesus, it's suppertime, don't be late.

Don't build your house on the things Jesus has taken away.
Jesus is building us a new house, our past is gone,
Jesus is our new day.

(Scriptural Reference: Hebrews 1:2, 3)
(Refer to **reference 25** on pg. 155 in the section of **Personal Notations and Thoughts** on God's creative power.)

CRUCIFXION SIDE FIRST

Friday is before Sunday, in the days of the week.
The one that shed His blood for us, has risen, the one we all seek.

In the seasons of our lives, we must go thru the cross,
crucifixion side first.
Then comes the resurrection side, after the worst.

If we truly love Jesus, on the cross we must put Him first.
What a glorious resurrection, after Satan has done His worst.

Satan used his power, he gave it his all; it wasn't enough.
Jesus looked straight at Satan, Jesus said from now on it's
going to get rough.

You can't give love, if you have no love to give.
You must give love if you truly want to live.

If we have a heart that is blackened by sin,
We can't walk in the light from the heart within.

We can't change the world when we pray,
Till we first give ourselves to God every minute, every day.

Jesus has risen: what a wonderful thing!
Think about that, doesn't that make you want to sing?

(Scriptural Reference: Mark 8:34-38)
(Refer to **reference 26** on pg. 155 in the section of **Personal Notations and Thoughts** on carrying the cross.)

THE QUESTION IS?

The Law was made to serve man, not man to serve the Law.
The way to escape our sin, that's what Jesus saw.

Man was made to serve God not God to serve man.
Jesus came to serve us, was always His plan.

Grace was given to man, not man given to grace.
God forgave us anyway, Jesus died in our place.

Love is God, did God give Himself to man?
Jesus died for us on the cross, even though man did it,
it was still God's plan.

Satan came to take man's life, and give nothing good in return.
If we listen to Satan, along with him we will burn.

Love serves all others, all others serve love.
Jesus came to lead us out of bondage, to a higher place above.

Man can wander in the desert forty years or more
without a clue.
From the beginning of time, the answer God knew.

(Scriptural Reference: Matthew 5:17-20)
(Refer to **reference 27** on pg. 156 in the section of **Personal Notations and Thoughts** on heart attitude and actions.)

THE END WHERE WE START

One Father God, one Jesus our Lord,
One Holy Spirit in one accord.

One in love, all for God's glory.
Love in Christ, is the rest of the story.

God sees all we do, be it good or bad,
Let your roots grow deep, live your life as though
Jesus is all you had.

If we wish to return to God, we must stop listening to Satan
the faker.
We begin in the garden with God as our maker.

Where you plant seed, is the area of your life that will grow.
If we plant our hearts in Jesus, we can reap much more
than we sow.

One world in Christ, full of His presence of heart.
The Spirit Jesus sent, the end where we start

(Scriptural Reference: Revelation 1:8)
(Refer to **reference 28** on pg. 156 in the section of **Personal Notations and Thoughts** on Jesus being the Beginning and the End of all matters.)

Lying

If we steal we are going to jail.
If we take instead of give we're bound to fail.

If you know someone that hasn't got any friends,
Help that person to make amends.

If we do what we can to be loving and kind,
We can give others a hand instead of a piece of our mind.

If we long to see the light just over the hill top,
Don't agree with a lie just tell them to stop.

If the one that is lying turns out to be you or me,
Ask Jesus to forgive you and please ask Jesus to forgive me.

(Scriptural Reference: 1 John 2:4)
(Refer to **reference 29** on pg. 156 in the section of **Personal Notations and Thoughts** on belonging to Jesus.)

FRUIT OF THE TREE

Don't be fooled, don't be deceived.
If we are too busy for God, His Spirit is grieved.

God knows if we are too busy for Him.
Man will leave himself out on a limb.

If we never have time for the Son of God,
The devil will rule in our life, and stomp us roughshod.

The Holy Spirit is always trying to help us grieve,
If we have no time for others, the Holy Spirit will leave.

If we tell the people that we know,
We have no time for them, we have to go.

God will love us anyway, if we have not time for the least
of these.
We will find ourselves standing in the forest alone,
unable to see the trees.

Don't look back to Sodom and Gomorrah.
Set your hand to the plow.
Go forward, give your heart to Jesus today,
the time is now.

(Scriptural References: Genesis 19:1-31; Proverbs 11:30; Luke 9:62)
(Refer to **reference 30** on pg. 156 in the section of **Personal Notations and Thoughts** on gaining wisdom.)

SWORD OF GOD

Let every man be a liar.
Jesus sets our hearts on fire.

God knows man is full of sin,
That's why He sent His next of kin.

There is only one Jesus that died for me.
Thank God for the completeness of trinity.

Salvation is given, by God only.
Ask for the Spirit, you won't be lonely.

Only Jesus can take away our pain.
To be without the Lord is quite insane.

If we are too busy to seek the Lord,
We will never possess God's life-saving double edged sword.

(Scriptural References: Ephesians 6:17; Hebrews 4:12; Revelation 1:16)
(Refer to **reference 31** on pg. 156 in the section of **Personal Notations and Thoughts** on the believer's weapon.)

FOLLOW THE MASTER

Jesus loves my enemy; He shows mercy to those I love indeed.
As we stand in the midst of the wilderness, Jesus gives
us what we need.

If we long to have a mansion, in the midst of Paradise on earth,
We must build our home with love, and forgive for all its worth.

Plant your seed in good ground, watch over it as it grows.
Put your trust in Jesus, Jesus is the way, follow Him as
He goes.

If we long to see others follow in the ways of God,
We must be willing to follow first even though people think we're odd.

If we are heading upstream we need to paddle a little faster,
If we long to see others follow in the way of the Master.

Even if in truth we are a little short, God can make us stand tall.
If we trust in Jesus, yes we can have it all.

(Scriptural Reference: Galatians 6:7, 8)
(Refer to **reference 32** on pg. 156 in the section of **Personal Notations and Thoughts** on reaping and sowing.)

SPIRIT WINGS

I often wonder why others don't see?
Just how wonderful Jesus is to you and me.

Don't you sometimes wish you could show, all people
how to love?
Introduce them to Jesus, with spirit wings of a dove.

Jesus has enough love to cover all the earth and more.
In the middle of God's garden like it was before.

When we walked with God before man took the fall,
To be like a child of God, when God was all.

We must be like children to receive God's best.
We must be like children to enter God's rest.

(Scriptural Reference: Psalm 37:4, 5)
(Refer to **reference 33** on the pg. 157 in the section of **Personal Notations and Thoughts** on delighting in the Lord.)

I

See

God

Book

Five

TO KNOW JESUS

God's purpose for mankind is not to end it right here,
But a new beginning with Jesus without fear.

God will purify the heavens and earth.
With fire He will create higher birth.

We can look forward to Jesus' return.
In the meantime His ways we should learn.

If we help others to see Jesus clearly,
Then they too will follow Jesus securely.

If we look straight up into Jesus' face,
And try our hardest to live by God's grace.

To know Jesus better is most important you see.
To be more like Jesus the best you can be.

Jesus is not finished making us better.
I suppose it's like putting a special, p.s. on the letter.

JESUS IS THE LIGHT

There is a place where Jesus has prepared for us to be,
A place with many mansions where our spirit can roam free.

I hear it is more wonderful then our hearts and minds can understand,
With endless things of wonder built by God's own hand.

Have faith and trust in Jesus, He has an inheritance for you.
This is only the beginning, Jesus isn't nearly through.

Jesus has done all things that are needed so far as I know.
Jesus isn't through with us we have a long way to go.

Take heart if we travel after Jesus in His way.
We will soon see the light of Jesus every day.

NEW LIFE

The man who loves His life will lose it or
He can give it up and God will use it.

Unless a single seed dies, it remains only one little seed.
The life given for others fill many a need.

When we give up our old life and let the Spirit of Jesus renew,
New life will spring up in the things that we do.

THE GREEN VALLEY

What does Jesus pray for us when we do His will?
Does He say follow me I know a way over this hill?

Does He say there is a green valley on the other side?
My Father is waiting with open arms stretched out wide.

Come quickly my children, there is room for you all there,
I'm going to make sure you all have plenty to share.

In the green valley life goes on forevermore.
We can't even imagine all the good things that are in store.

You don't have to pay for anything there.
Jesus paid with His life to show how much He does care.

Don't worry Jesus has risen, He is alive.
He is waiting in the green valley for us to arrive.

In the green valley there is no darkness, only light,
That comes from God what a beautiful sight.

The lamb and the lion will lie down together,
Nothing will harm them no not ever.

All poison will be gone in the green valley, everyone gives,
The children will play unafraid by the hole where the asp lives.

THE LIGHTHOUSE

There is this place called the lighthouse,
I've seen Jesus there.
Jesus is the lighthouse where people come to share.

Come to the lighthouse if you have lost your way.
Come to the lighthouse if you just want to pray.

If your ship is on a collision course and
heading for the rocks upon the shore,
That is what the lighthouse is shining brightly for.

Look up to the lighthouse to guide you safely in.
Jesus is the lighthouse to steer you away from sin.

The lighthouse stands on solid rock,
looking for man tossed upon the sea.
When all the things of darkness have passed away,
Jesus will still be.

YOUR TRIAL

You are on trial for your life the verdict is already in.
Jesus Christ has taken your case and wiped away your sin.

The judge is Jesus' Father the highest authority anywhere.
Jesus has pleaded our case in love and reverent care.

The opposition says we are guilty and makes a very good case.
The judge says, "I see no sin while looking at Jesus' face."

With Jesus as our counsel, the opposition cannot win.
We only have to obey God and give up all our sin.

We don't have to feel guilty and live in despair,
Even though our trails are not over, God's love is everywhere.

Our advocate defender is Jesus the judge's Son.
He has paid full penalty, your case has already been won.

You can't even pay your fine; put your money in your pocket.
You can't be tried for a case no longer on the docket.

Those of you standing in the back of the court,
step forward you can be forgiven too.
The Judge on Jesus' testimony is ready to forgive you.

Step forward and ask to be forgiven of all your sins.
Your Advocate Judge wants to say you win.

LIFE FOR JESUS

Jesus can lift you when you fall down.
If you live your life for Jesus, you will receive a crown.

If you walk with Jesus filled with the light of the Lord,
Speak words of wisdom out of the two-edged sword.

117

With an open heart for others, ready to fill every need,
God will plant in you life giving seed.

Don't even worry what it is you will speak,
There is life in the Word you can turn the other cheek.

Having what we need is all about giving what we have to others.
God remembers us when we remember our brothers.

We will walk in power when we don't shift the blame.
How we treat others, God promises to treat us the same.

Where Jesus has walked, allows us to live without blame.
We can be forgiven in Jesus' name.

WALK WITH JESUS

The Bible is God's living Word.
There is more power here then you've ever heard.

When Jesus with power spoke the words of life,
The power of God cut like a double-edged knife.

Lazarus rose up when Jesus gave a soft shout.
Jesus spoke the word and Lazarus came out.

Lazarus walked with Jesus once again.
If we walk with Jesus we are free from sin.

The Bible is the only book we need,
Let's walk with Jesus and plant some seed.

Let's walk with Jesus and on the way,
Help someone to have a nice day.

Let's walk with Jesus, let's open the book.
Jesus is on every page we look.

Eagles fly high and have powerful wings.
More than that is what faith in God brings.

I SEE GOD

I see God everywhere I look.
It takes God's trees to make a book.

It takes God's trees to make man's money.
It takes God's bees to make God's honey.

To make anything man has made,
It takes God's foundations to be laid.

It takes God to make a flower,
Without water there would be no shower.

What on earth would man do without God's love?
Without God who would make the dove?

I see God when I look at your face.
You have life because of God's grace.

Man is striving to go to Mars,
I see God's hand in millions of stars.

Man cannot see all that God has made.
Without God's love, man's plan would not have been laid.

I see God when I get on my knees to pray,
We can be forgiven it is God's way.

119

ENDLESS LOVE

Jesus we pray send the Holy Spirit from above.
Life with Christ is endless love.

In heaven there is no loneliness to be found,
We will feel warm and loved with God all around.

No more tears of sorrow,
No end to our days, no more to tomorrow.

No more goodbyes, no more darkness at all.
The light of love will smash down the wall.

If we feel lost it does not have to be.
Jesus opened the way to eternity.

Although it's true we all are sinners,
It's in God's plan for us to be winners.

We can have it all, Jesus is the way.
Invite Jesus in when you kneel and pray.

Jesus is alive forevermore.
He is waiting for us to step through the door.

HOW WE TREAT OTHERS

Love is how we treat people in spite of how they treat us.
Love is waiting on others even though they wouldn't let us get on the
bus.

Love is building others up even when they're tearing you apart unfair.
Love is standing alone when the Philistines left you bound in despair.

Love is giving to others when they are stealing from us.
Love is forgiving others when they have broken your trust.

120

Love is what Jesus is in every <u>loving</u> way.
Love is choosing to believe in Jesus to live each <u>new</u> <u>day</u>.

Love is facing your troubles and making them go away.
Love is encouraging each other and agreeing when we pray.

Love is getting off the bus that is going down the one way street the wrong way.
Telling others about Jesus, tell them to get off Satan's bus and pray.

Love is knowing Jesus and standing up for what is right.
Love is giving up your sleep to pray for a sick child all night.

Love is Jesus, paying with His life that only He could do.
God's ways are far above our ways, thank you Jesus we can depend on You.

YOUR SECRET GARDEN

We live here on earth with a secret garden within.
Jesus has planted seeds in our heart to save us from our sin.

If we accept Jesus into our garden, He plants blessings that grow.
Others need Jesus, even everyone we know.

Does Jesus live in your garden where love and goodness grows?
Jesus is the only way to seeds of hope we will ever know.

To keep weeds from growing wild and over running your soul,
Keep Jesus close to your heart should always be our goal.

Once the weeds of hate are gone, don't look back towards the sin.
Then we will never become entangled with hopelessness again.

Let Jesus plant in your garden in good soil all the things
that come from above.
Let the sun shine all through your life that comes from God above.

JESUS HEALED YOU

Jesus' blood has healed you.
Jesus' blood makes all things new.

If we complain it goes to our shame,
Cuz Jesus has healed you.

Jesus has unlocked the door, nothing but good things
are in store.
Cuz Jesus has healed you.

If we have troubles, our problems coming in doubles,
Remember Jesus has healed you.

If we hang on to the past, let go, it won't last,
Cuz Jesus has healed you.

If someone offended you, well that just won't do,
Cuz Jesus has healed you.

If we are poor by the world's estimation, get your train
moving out of the station,
Cuz Jesus has healed you.

If we don't have a clue, kneel down and pray
all the way through,
Cuz Jesus has healed you.

If we are too busy with important things to do,
Let's try to remember, it was Jesus who healed you.

HEAVEN'S GATE

Oh Lord you love your people much it is plain to see.
You bless us with Your love, our souls You have set free.

Teach us Lord not to fear anything man can do.
Put in us all the fear of God, we know your Word is true.

Let us teach Your Word according to your will.
Let us turn that mountain into a little hill.

Give us each day only what we can bear,
In love and kindness with others to share.

Show us how dear Lord that we can forgive the other guy,
And all mankind will come to you by and by.

Lord, we long to walk in the garden once more,
As Adam and Eve did so long before.

To walk in the garden to be at your side,
And no longer from you would we try to hide.

It would be so nice to feel no more hate
As we all strolled together through heaven's gate.

GROW IN LOVE

God does not want us to sneak into heaven over the back fence
in the dark. He wants us to go in the front.

Lord, make me a blessing to someone today.
Give me directions as I kneel to pray.

For those walking in darkness in the middle of the day,
Let's help them to see the light when we kneel and pray.

Let's pray together with raptors of love.
Lord, please send salvation from Your throne above.

If you are sick in any way,
Send for Doctor Jesus, it's time to pray.

Ask Jesus to lighten each heart.
Now today is the time to start.

Bow down your head, ask God to forgive.
You will never die, Jesus wants you to live.

In the early morning at the dawn of light,
The sunshine chases away the dark of night.

It's important for life here in earth,
The Spirit within is of much greater worth.

The weather within is most important indeed.
The Holy Spirit is what we need.

The fullness of what God has to give,
Is what we need to grow and live.

We must add to our diet food from above,
Until we can say what God created we love.

ROMANS CHAPTER TWELVE

Love is chopping wood to keep others warm,
when they are giving us the cold shoulder.
Love is making a choice to love our brothers,
even though they sold us naked and colder.

Love is helping others up even though they were the ones that
knocked us down.
Love is praying for others, even and including the bully of the town.

Love is Jesus saying, "Forgive them Father for they
know not what they do."
Jesus help us to walk and talk and forgive others,
being more and more like You.

Such love we never gave or knew,
Till Jesus to us was made really true.

If we invite Jesus to our pity party, He will give our party a different
tone.
We don't have a right to have a pity party all by our self alone.

If we love Jesus who died for us, we have no right to feel sorry
for us, for shame.
Jesus has all the right to love us; on self-pity we have no claim.

Jesus died and buried our sins in the place where they belong forever.
Then Jesus rose up in power, forgetting our sins
to respect our sins never.

HE IS COMING

Jesus is coming back; He will be coming in great power.
Will we be ready to meet our Savior in that hour?

Will our lamp be filled with oil when Jesus comes for His bride?
Will we be ashamed and turn our face to hide?

When the last trumpet sounds, will we rally to the call?
Or, will we not be ready with our back to the wall?

When our Savior arrives will we be ready to go in?
Or, will our garment be soiled and stained with sin?

When Jesus comes for us, will we be hard at work helping others?
Or, will we be fast asleep not caring for our brothers?

Don't worry, what's impossible for man,
When it comes to the impossible, Jesus can.

Let's all be ready when Jesus comes again.
He will say, "Good and faithful servant come right in."

GOD MADE MOTHERS

The mother of my Savior gave birth to Jesus her Son.
All the universe gave testament that Jesus is the One.

A proud Father God watched over the one He sent to earth.
The purity of God came to man through virgin birth.

Mothers love and care for their children and help them grow strong.
And pray that all their days on earth will be happy and long.

Every mother on earth does a wonderful thing for man.
God took a rib and carried out His plan.

God did a wonderful thing when He created a mother.
No intelligent child would want any other.

Thank you God, You did not stop when You made man.
You went on to make a woman to complete Your plan.

Thank you God for taking a rib and making a woman so nice.
I suppose it couldn't be any better even if You did that twice.

HAPPY MOTHERS

Happy Mother's day to all the ladies that have no children by man.
Yet have lots of children by the grace and love of God's plan.

In the garden, Adam and Eve first walked with God in the cool.
Not knowing that Satan was evil and looking for who he could fool.

Now we wonder what is coming is coming to pass and what is going on today.
God is always walking with those that love Him and kneel and pray.

Beyond this earth is the expanse of heaven that goes on forevermore.
When we get to heaven, we can't imagine the wonder that is in store.

FATHER GOD

A father is someone we try to be.
He is the one who leads His family to victory.

A father is one with all his ducks in a row,
He is really a very good person to know.

A father leads His children by example in love.
He never treats his children unfairly by push and shove.

A father is always there when his family needs him night or day.
He keeps watch on his family when at work or play.

I do know one who can handle all we need.
He is our Father God, who is a Father indeed.

OUR UNCOMMON SAVIOR

It was common for Jesus to walk 50 miles to make a friend.
It was common for His disciples to be exhausted at day's end.

It was common for Jesus to pray through the night.
It was common for His disciples to be confused full of fright.

It was common for Jesus to be way ahead of others.
If we love Jesus, He will call us His brothers.

It was common for Jesus to forgive His enemies when they did Him
wrong.
There is no weakness in Jesus, He is totally strong.

It was common for Jesus to see straight through a lie.
Sometimes when I think about Him, I just want to cry.

It was common for Jesus to look up to heaven,
When Judas betrayed Him then there were eleven.

It was common for Jesus to know exactly what to say.
Now follow after Jesus, children, for that is the way.

It was common for Jesus to give to those in need.
It was common for Jesus, 5,000 to feed.

It was common for Jesus to give His life's blood for us.
Our uncommon Savior went to the cross without making a fuss.

Jesus was thinking of us in man's darkest hour.
Jesus is living for us in uncommon power.

FREE US LORD

Bind me Lord to Thy purpose and will.
Let the fear within be quiet and still.

Teach me Lord to return Your love,
So others may see Your light from above.

Oh dear precious Lord, please work through me,
So we can serve You for all eternity.

Let my will be yours Lord, all through the day,
So the bindings of Satan may be taken away.

Help me to be Yours and pray on bended knee,
So those that walk proud, Your face may yet see.

LAST HOUR

Lord build in me a strong heart, filled with Your power.
Give me strength to do the work until the very last hour.

Lord sweep all the darkness out of me, fill me with your light of love.
Fill my heart with Your things that come from above.

Take from us Lord, the things of this world that fill us with hate.
Oh, please Lord do this before it becomes too late.

Take all the things that separate us from You.
Please build a wall around us that can't be broken through.

Lord, show us where Your will lies within us all,
So we may stand up straight and tall.

Give Your hand to us of the things You are giving,
So we may lead others where Your people are living.

THANK YOU LORD

Oh Lord on this day you have given us to enjoy,
We thank you Lord for each girl and boy.

Lord give us a thankful heart all year long.
Make our faith in you loving, helpful, and strong.

All the loveliness you have made for our eyes to behold,
You have made for our eyes to behold is so precious
it could not for any price be sold.

In this land of plenty, Lord help us to share,
For your glory Lord, let us show others we care.

Give us peace and love in you to share.
Help us show others that love like yours is more than rare.

129

Help us put on your armor and hold your sword tight,
And walk straight in your Word by the splendor of your light.

It's by your power and for you we live.
If we would have more than we must give.

Mutual things are not what we should desire,
But the spiritual things that lift others higher.

HARVEST

Our entire life, spiritually we all need to grow.
Our entire life Jesus is the one we need to know.

Today Lord, give us at least one that we can tell about you,
We pray Lord can you give us at least two?

Lord, please don't get angry, could you please maybe send three?
If four wouldn't be too many, maybe that is what the number could be.

Lord, I know a lot of people that really need you,
Could you please send a dozen or maybe twenty-two?

Lord, give us the wisdom to know what to pray.
Tell us Lord how you would have us lead others in Your way.

Lord, put us to work in this the last hour.
Send us out to work in your harvest in uncommon power.

IT'S SO

If you have lost something, try not to be sad.
For God once lost the only Son He ever had.

That would be tragic, but on the third day
Jesus rose up from the place that He lay.

His disciples noticed that their hearts burned within
When in the presence of Jesus they had been.

He opened the Scriptures to them so the Bible said,
"Jesus has risen, the Master is not dead."

This is all true in my heart I know,
If you seek God, you will see that it is so.

(Scriptural References: Luke 24:13-53; 1 Corinthians 8:1-3)

NOT WORTHY

Lord, we hate the sin that we see
In your presence in the spirit we would be.

We love sinners, but not what they do.
We wish we could be more like you.

Lord, we know there is much you would give us if we could bear,
The power you would give us, you will always be there.

Although we are not worthy to be like you,
The blood of Jesus is what we cling to.

PLANTING GOD'S SEED

There is a song that's sweeter than can be sung by a bird.
You won't find it in this world, but in God's holy Word.

The loving words of Jesus can fill your heart so full of love.
He can send to you a Comforter like the wings of a dove.

If we would not clutter our life with things that we don't need,
And spend more time in the harvest of God sowing holy seed.

We can find in God's work all that we need,
To bring long life, peace, and happiness planting God's seed.

THOSE THAT ASK

God is love this is understood,
He gave us salvation as only He would.

Through Jesus the works of life flow,
To those that ask and wish to know.

GRACE OF LOVE

Oh dear Lord, Your grace of love is all we need,
To sing your praise with utmost speed.

Lord, you said by our fruits we shall be known,
For by your perfect love we will be shown.

It is such a thrill Lord to do things your way,
To bow before you and softly pray.

If our praise does not reach your throne above,
The very stones will cry out with love.

For we must be in tune with you,
To have peace in the things we do.

NEW WINE
(Matthew Nine)

Jesus never charged when He healed you.
No that is not something that Jesus would do.

Jesus thought no evil of others He met,
Of what perfect example He set.

Jesus had power to forgive all sin.
Jesus gave life; it is not something you win.

The Master came and sat among sinners.
Oh praise God, for now we are winners.

As we wait for Jesus, now we fast.
We know this world, it will not last.

Before we knew Jesus, we thirsted indeed.
And now we have all the new wine we need.

NEW COVENANT

The Bible mentions wild honey,
We shouldn't have a love for money.

The city of God has golden streets,
We must be careful of a love for sweets.

We have so much to thank God for,
He could not love you anymore.

He loves you now as He did then,
From the beginnings of time until the end.

It's so easy to see God's hand on you,
He stills the storms that you pass through.

The seed is the Word of God,
To prepare the field you must till the sod.

"The time is coming," declares the Lord.
It says in the Bible which is our sword.

"I will make a new covenant with those that follow me.
I will write in their hearts what I want them to be."

DON'T LIE

Don't worry what to eat or drink.
Don't even imagine what others might think.

You may think it's strange for certainty it's so.
God does things differently than people here below.

If you want God to draw close to you,
You must not do the things that some do.

You must walk straight, you must not lie,
If you want to go to heaven when you die.

Death is swallowed up in victory as you know.
So be sure you're saved before you go.

Calvin Alford

NO TIME

No time for Satan, what he has taken.
It's time to serve Jesus, the world is about to be shaken.

No time to give Satan the time of the day.
There is no time to serve Satan, it's time to pray.

There is no time like the present to tell others about Jesus that's
coming from above.
It's time to tell our neighbors about our Savior that is coming in love.

No time in the past has God loved us anymore.
Read your Bible and see the blessings God has in store.

God loved those that love Him in truth for His glory.
He wants to comfort the hurting; in the Bible is the rest of the story.

There may yet be time to give God's message to the lost.
The good news about Jesus and why he had to hang on the cross.

There may yet be time to forgive the pain of the past.
And tell all the people how long eternity is going to last.

MY GOD

My God is one of a kind, there is no other.
My God is one of a kind; please listen to me my brother.

My God is a jealous God; He wants the best for me.
My God is a jealous God; He wants me to be the best that I can be.

My God loves me and my God loves you too.
Do you know my God? I will introduce Him to you

135

All have sinned (*Romans 3:23*),
falling short of the glory of God.
For the wages of sin is death,
but the free Gift of God is eternal life
in Christ Jesus, our Lord (*Romans 6:23*).
God loves you. He demonstrated His love
towards us in that while we were yet sinners,
Christ died for us (*Romans 5:8*).
That if you confess with your mouth
Jesus is Lord and believe in your heart
that God raised Him from the dead, you
will be saved (*Romans 10:9, 10*).

GOD GIVES

Lord we have peace and joy in serving You.
We have that something the world never knew.

Your glorious light shines in those that love You.
It's there for the world to see in the things that they do.

They each have a gift sent from God directly to them.
To build others in the Body, maybe a song or a hymn.

We can have for keeps what God gives us today,
If we will love others and give it away.

Now it may sound strange if we give it some thought.
God doesn't ask much of us, but what He gives is a lot.

The  Way

to

Life

INTRODUCTION

The following poems by Cal were part of a series of poems showing the way to life. It is clear that the heart of the poet is to make sure that people understand that there is no life outside of Jesus Christ and His redemption. This series of poems also reveal every believer's heavenly calling as they look forward to Jesus' future reign.

    This set of inspired poems will clearly give the reader a chance to meditate, allowing for understanding to dawn upon the seeking heart and encouragement to captivate the wandering, restless soul.

Love is what Jesus is in every <u>loving way</u>.
Love is choosing to believe in Jesus to live each <u>new day</u>.

Love is facing your trouble and making them go away.
Love is encouraging each other and agreeing when we pray.

Love is getting off the bus that is going down
the one way street the wrong way.
Telling others about Jesus, tell them to get off Satan's bus and pray.

Love is knowing Jesus and standing up for what is right.
Love is giving up your sleep to pray for a sick child all night.

Love is Jesus, paying with His life that only He could do.
God's ways are far above our ways,
thank you Jesus, we can depend on you.

God has work for us; His yoke is never heavy but is <u>light</u>.
With love, God has filled us to make us ready, it's God's <u>fight</u>.

When we are in love with ourselves, that love always has
conditions to meet.
We can't give all God gives us, even if we give love to everyone
we greet.

Give some love away, God will give you more.
Give some love away, be an open door.

God's love will find you even in the pit of despair.
God's love will find you; you can't hide from Him anywhere.

If we ask, God will fill us with love that will not shy away or fade.
Father God sent His beloved Son to earth for us, full price He paid.

Jesus found us broke and far from home, He paid our way,
the entire cost.
Do you feel loved when you think of what Jesus did for us
when we were lost?

All things will soon pass away: the old evil nature
will be seen no more.
The new spiritual nature in keeping the unity in love,
stepping thru eternity's door.

If God was first in our lives, we would no longer need
hospitals, doctors, medicines that sometime make us
sicker than when we got sick.

We would be so in tune with each other,
that we wouldn't argue or fight.

There would be no need for lawyers or judges.

God would fix all things before they got to be a problem.

We would all be as one. What's the point of arguing with ourselves?

If we listened to Jesus, there would be no sick, there would be no overweight, we would not forget names, dates, or anything that Jesus taught us.

We would never be in pain; we would never be cold or too hot.

We wouldn't need insurance if we listened to Jesus,
We would need each other, we all need Jesus.

Do you hunger and thirst for God?

(Scriptural Reference: Revelation 21:1-8)

We the favored of God, the remnant, spreading God's Word.
Telling others the Good News of salvation in love that we heard.

We care for each other because God loved us first.
By the blood of the Lamb we can overcome the worst.

The Lord leads us thru; He will not leave us without hope.
The Lord cleanses us inside and out with His blood not soap.

God makes us a way to be lifted up to freedom thru Him.
If we keep following Jesus, our light will not grow dim.

By Jesus' stripes we are healed from all of our sin.
If we know Jesus, we don't have to go back to the past again.

Those that love Jesus have found the way.
They will have light to continue each day.

Don't let the earthly flesh keep you earthbound.
Let the Spirit of Jesus set you free, don't let yourself down.

Jesus loves you without condemnation. Man's life is like the ripple on a
pond.
To live a long time on earth is good; to spend eternity with Jesus goes
on and beyond.

Jesus doesn't compromise. He's no respecter of persons, He's just.
Jesus is the one that does all things well, Jesus the one to trust.

Jesus walked without fault all His days on earth.
Jesus, the firstborn of God's Spirit, perfect from birth.

Men are not perfect; some are filled with pride by choice.
It's time to seek the Son of God and listen to His voice.

Let's all head for higher ground, Jesus will be leading.
In the pages of the Bible, it's the book we should be reading.

God wants people that are not perfect to follow His leading.
When all the fields are planted and watered, we will have the harvest
we are needing.

*(**Scriptural Reference:** Galatians 5:17)*

Sin makes us angry, love makes us strong.
Jesus is coming again, and it won't be too long.

Sin makes us weak, the Law man cannot master.
The grace of God is the only thing to run boldly after.

Don't get sidetracked on detours that lead to sin's dark light of day.
Follow life with all care; let it not slip from your grasp and fade away.

141

Would you invest in death that forever gives no return?
Our flesh wants to lead, yet can't follow the truth or learn.

We are running in a race, we all want to win.
We will go on much faster, free from all sin.

Let no desire lead us away from life's fullness of praise.
Let the path of your feet be established far from evil ways.

I know this man that said only Jesus loves me.
He cried when he realized only Jesus can set us free.

Jesus can overcome any sorrow or pain.
Only the blood of Jesus covers, no sin will remain.

With no hope of living, trust Jesus to restore life,
sing a new song.
Only Jesus brings life to where death has been so long.

When praying for Jesus to come on the scene,
Pray with a heart that is striving to be clean.

Adam and Eve chose the way of the good and evil tree.
Jesus said, "I am the way, the truth," with me life will be.

Because Jesus lives, you shall live, He paid the cost.
The sweetness of God's honey is hidden from the lost.

Jesus, the Tree of Life stands forever in victory's light.
With Jesus as our teacher, salvation is never out of sight.

Listen to Jesus' words, be doers after the Heavenly Father up above.
Where Jesus has gone before, is the way we must follow in love.

Eyes lifted upwards in praise of a Savoir God rising.
God's heaven is filled with such singing and praying.

Learn to like what you don't like and it won't bother you anymore.
Learn to forgive all others, it will open heaven's golden door.

We can't act like the devil and take control over him at the same time.
We can't be a friend of the world and escape our fate while committing
a crime.

If we choose to turn away from Jesus, we are free to make that choice.
We will be justly rewarded according to the way we listen to God's
voice.

The way that Jesus went was not the fallen way of sin.
If Jesus told us once, He has forgiven us all again.

Those who believe in Jesus, the works Jesus does, He will do.
Jesus has gone to the Father to prepare for greater works in you.

Ask what you will in Jesus' loving name,
Keeping in mind, the reason that Jesus came.

The way of life shines brighter than all the stars above.
Jesus is the brightest star; He came willingly for us in love.

Keep your heart in joy above all else, guarding your walk on the way.
Loving the right direction, look straight ahead, choose carefully what
you say.

Don't let glitter for self pull you away from your goal.
Don't listen to Satan's lies; he has only what he stole.

If you have a bad attitude and complain, you are heading in the wrong direction.
Look in your mirror and try to reflect and see Christ's reflection.

God did not call us to minister to ourselves in a self-seeking direction.
Jesus told Peter to get thee behind me Satan, life-changing correction.

Guard your thoughts with actions that speak well of your mind.
God sees us all the time, a record is being kept of our actions in kind.

When we are driving and pass a police car we are careful not to speed.
We need to be careful; God did not write all the books that we read.

We are going to go thru some tough times with or without God's love.
It's our choice do we want to go down or be lifted up to heaven above?

Jesus went thru with His hands nailed to the cross of His own will.
His tormentors had a choice, ask forgiveness of God or forever pay their bill.

Staying in the Spirit, you walk in power.
When you are in the flesh it's Satan's strongest hour.

If we say we love God, but don't read His Bible, His letter to us,
It's like wanting to go somewhere, yet not getting on the bus.

As hard as we try, we can't live thru trying to earn.
If we study God's Word and follow Jesus, we can learn.

We can pray to the Father, for a hunger and a thirst.
God will give us all that we ask if we put Him first.

I've heard it said the Apostle Paul had camel's knees.
Praying in love for others as busy as honey bees.

Be like little children, be the hope that the child needs.
Be more and more like Jesus, motivate others to plant seeds.

Spots on a leopard cannot be rearranged by man's will.
The sins of the flesh, Jesus can remove; He has paid the bill.

Why be spotted by sin that God has removed with His love.
Alone, we haven't a <u>chance</u>.
Jesus is waiting to take us home after the <u>last</u> <u>dance</u>.

Rejoice and be happy, be filled with laughter.
God's house will be filled with love from rafter to rafter.

No matter how far we have gone down the road in our sin,
Jesus can remove stains of sin to pure white once again.

Love is the detergent that out lasts the night.
Love is the soap that makes a sinner pure white.

Bold is the color as bright as the sun.
We can be clean, Jesus will forgive us. His colors don't run.

Love is permanent, Jesus will not ever die.
We can be with Jesus forever you and I.

The blind leading the blind will surely lead to trouble.
Those with blinded minds fall into a pit of misery double.

The veil over the mind can only be lifted by trusting in Jesus overall.
With Jesus leading, it doesn't matter if the enemy seems ten feet tall.

If we be determined in faith to follow the Lord, that is a good start.
The battle ground is in the mind that is ruled by the heart.

What is seen is passing away, yet the inward man is renewed day by day.
The glory that is coming is eternal light of love that will never pass away.

Heart sight is the best; it's much clearer of a higher kind.
If you see Jesus in others, you're winning the battle of the mind.

Love covers a multitude of sins above and beyond our ability to.
Don't keep track of the bad things others do to you.
Rejoice in God's love for you.

Love build us up, anger pulls us down till we lose our way.
Love is steadfast, love sticks with us, makes us smile each day.

Personal
Notations and
Thoughts

FAITH

If we look close, we can see standing in heaven, upright and steady, a beautiful white cross. Its light is brilliant, shinning with light touching all corners of the world, filling believers with hope, faith, and love. These three virtues surround the cross where His blood entirely cleans and purifies as it covers all who come into the light of the cross.

Let us give thanks and receive the gifts of the Lord Jesus Christ. Let us live in peace with all the world that was certainly created by God.

If you love Jesus, you need have no fear of the coming trouble. Children, if you know Jesus, He knows where the sun rises and sets. He knows where the pot of gold is at the end of the rainbow. He can lead you to it. You can have a share on all the riches that God wants to give you.

LIGHT OF LOVE

Keeping your eyes on Jesus is like following a bright light of love through the dark woods of life. We must never look back or to either side for if we do, we may find when we again look for the light of love, it will still be there, but we can no longer see it in our blinded condition. Only through keeping watch with persistence can we hope to keep on seeing with love. If we wish to learn to read and write, we go to school. If we wish to paint, we go to art school. If we wish to learn to love then we should read our Bible and go where we can to be closer to people that are filled with the love of God. We should want to learn to love through loving, and we will be aware of the light of love in our hearts.

JESUS HEALED PAUL

I can't imagine Paul on land being happy about a snake biting him, but I can see him nonchalantly shaking it off into the fire and praising Jesus. I can see him being content even though he had just been ship-wrecked and was now soaking wet, but smiling, as he warmed himself by the fire. He had just prayed and God spared the lives of everyone on the ship. Paul didn't stay by the fire to warm himself, he ended up ministering to lots of people.

Paul hurried to wait on all who had need, being careful to let the people know that they were the guests of Jesus' mercy. God gave Paul everything he needed, and on top of that, he gave Paul what he asked for too. Paul didn't stand around; rather, he seized the opportunity to give glory to Jesus because Jesus had healed him.

LIVING WATER

In *John 4:15*, Jesus gave her living water and many believed in Him because of the woman's testimony. In *John 4:29*, we see how lots of people know us on the outside, but Jesus knows us inside out. We can talk to Jesus about anything. There isn't anything he doesn't know about us. In *John 3:5* and *3:22*, we see Jesus baptizing with the Holy Spirit. According to *John 4:24, 32*, and *35*, many things Jesus did was shocking and completely ripped away the walls of unbelief and self-righteousness, and destroyed hatred and replaced it with hope and faith.

In *John 3:5*, our Lord again insists that a new birth is necessary, and explains that it must be an inward and a spiritual birth. It must not be only of water in regard to outward baptism, but there must be an inward baptism where a proper appreciation of what it means to be a member of Christ's kingdom, which involves the Spirit.

POETIC INSPIRATION

1) Right means morally good. The blood of Jesus makes man right. Right means to "restore." Jesus gave His life to restore us to life. At Jesus' birth Satan's power and control were disrupted. In the desert Jesus overcame the devil's temptations and at the resurrection He defeated Satan's ultimate weapon: Death. Eventually Satan will be constrained forever (*Revelation 20:10*), and evil will no longer pervade the earth. Jesus has complete power and authority over Satan and all His forces.

2) A friend is a person with whom one is on terms of mutual affection and respect. JESUS is a FRIEND indeed.

3) Love has become a mixed up term with little meaning. Today people are still confused about love. Love is the greatest of all human qualities, and it is an attribute of God Himself (*1 John 4:8*). Love involves unselfish service to others, to show it gives evidence that you care. Faith is the foundation and content of God's message, hope is the attitude and focus, and love is the action when faith and hope are in line. You are free to love completely because you understand how God loves.

4) God is no respecter of persons. Jesus loves us all, but when it comes to wickedness, we bring consequences on ourselves and eventually wickedness will correct each us.

5) Jesus' food is to do the will of the One who sent Him and to finish His work.

6) The meaning of "saved" is to rescue, to keep from danger or harm or capture, to free from the power of sin or its spiritual consequences.

7) Throughout the Bible we find this phrase, "Do not be afraid." God wasn't trying to scare the people. He was showing His mighty power so the Israelites would know He was the true God and would therefore obey Him. If they would do this, He would make

His power available to them. God wants us to follow Him out of love rather than fear. To overcome fear, we must think more about God's love. *First John 4:18* says, "Perfect love casts out fear."

8) We cannot imagine all that God has in store for us, both in this life and for eternity. He will create a new heaven and a new earth (*Isaiah 65:17; Revelation 21:1*). We will live with Him forever, and until then His Holy Spirit comforts and guides us. Knowing the wonderful and eternal future that awaits us gives us hope and courage to press on in this life, to endure hardships and to avoid giving into temptation. This world is not all there is. The best is yet to come.

9) We are under God's orders to eliminate any thoughts, practices, or possessions that hinder our devotion to Him. Do as God commands, you will have victory. Give open and honest prayer to God.

10) Don't ignore needed change in your life (*Acts 13:50*). A changed life is the result of true repentance (*Matthew 3:8*).

11) Jesus says that if we truly love God and our neighbor, we will naturally keep the commandments. This is looking at God's Law positively; rather, than worrying about all we should not do. We should concentrate on all we can do to show our love for God and to others.

Lack of love is often easy to justify, even though it is never right. Our neighbor is anyone of any race, creed, or social background who is in need, and love means acting to meet the person's need. Wherever you live, there are needy people close by. There is no good reason for refusing to help.

Rather than trying to force your plans on God, try to discover His plan for you.

12) When we trust in Christ, we make an exchange—our sin for His righteousness. Our sin was poured into Christ at His crucifixion. His righteousness is poured into us at our conversion. This is what Christians mean by Christ's atonement for sin. In the world bartering only works when two people exchange goods of relatively equal value. But, God offers to trade His righteousness

for our sin—something of immeasurable worth for something completely worthless. How grateful we should be for His kindness to us.

Everything belongs to God. Some time back Satan stole from God. If we belong to God, everything Satan stole belongs to us. God is putting all His enemies at Jesus' feet.

If you like to win, the Bible says we need to be a servant of others. Serving God is a win-win.

13) What kind of God does nature reveal? Nature shows us a God of might, intelligence, and intricate detail; a God of order and beauty; a God who controls powerful forces: that is general revelation, as well as special revelation (the Bible and the coming of Jesus). Through such revelation, we learn about God's love and forgiveness, as well as the promise of eternal life. God has graciously given us both sources that we might fully believe in Him.

14) The Christian's most powerful resource is communion with God through prayer. The results are often greater than we thought were possible. Some people see prayer as a last resort to be tried when all else fails. This approach is backwards. Prayer should come first because God's power is infinitely greater than ours. It only makes sense to rely on it—especially because God encourages us to do so.

Some of us are thinking it was just an accidental stroke of good luck in the case of Elijah praying, but I don't believe anything happens by accident. Elijah was in the middle of God's will.

15) In *Genesis 6:3*, it mentions that man's days will be a 120 years. God was allowing the people of Noah's day 120 years to change their sinful ways. God shows His great patience with us as well. He is giving us time to quit living our way and begin living His way, the way He shows us in His Word. While 120 years seems like a long time, eventually the time ran out and the floodwaters swept across the earth. Your time also may be running out. Turn to God to seek forgiveness of sins. You can't see the stopwatch of God's patience, and there is no bargaining for additional time.

16) Jesus' words in *John 14:1-3* show that the way to eternal life, though unseen, is secure—as secure as your trust in Jesus. He has already prepared the way to eternal life. The only issue that may still be unsettled is your willingness to believe.

There are a few verses in Scripture that describe eternal life, but these few verses are rich with promises. Here Jesus says, "I am going there to prepare a place for you, and I will come back." We can look forward to eternal life because Jesus has promised it to all who believe in Him. Although the details of eternity are unknown, we need not fear because Jesus is preparing for us, and will spend eternity with us.

17) In *Matthew 25:1-13*, this parable is about a wedding. On the wedding day the bridegroom went to the bride's house for the ceremony, then the bride and groom, along with a great procession returned to the groom's house where a feast took place, often lasting a full week. These ten virgins were waiting to join the procession, and they hoped to take part in the wedding banquet, but when the groom didn't come at the expected time, five of them were out of lamp oil. By the time they had purchased extra oil, it was too late to join the feast. When Jesus returns to take His people to heaven, we must be ready. Spiritual preparation cannot be bought or borrowed at the last minute. Our relationship with God must be our own.

18) When someone gives you a gift, do you say, "That's very nice. Now how much do I owe you?" No, the appropriate response to a gift is thank you. Yet, how often do Christians, even after they have been given the gift of salvation, feel obligated to try to work their way to God? Because our salvation and even our faith are gifts, we should respond with gratitude, praise, and joy.

19) Jesus used the term "Living Water" in *John 4:10* to indicate eternal life. In *John 7:38*, He uses the term to refer to the Holy Spirit. The two scriptural references go together. However, when the Holy Spirit is accepted, He brings eternal life. Jesus teaches more about the Holy Spirit in *John* chapters *14* and 16. The Holy Spirit empowered Jesus' followers at Pentecost (*Acts 2*), and has since been available to all who believe in Jesus as Savior.

20) In *Leviticus 22:19-25* the animals with defects were not accepted as sacrifices because they did not represent God's holy nature. Furthermore, the animal had to be without blemish in order to foreshadow the perfect, sinless life of Jesus Christ. When we give our best time, talent, and treasure to God rather than what is tarnished or common, we show the true meaning of worship and testify to God's supreme worth.

21) Jesus is both David's root and offspring. As the Creator of all, Jesus existed long before David. As a human, He was one of David's direct descendants, as the Messiah, He is the Bright Morning Star, the Light of salvation to all.

22) "Discipline" comes from the word, "disciple." Jesus teaches about the cost of being a disciple.
Disciple of Jesus (*Matthew 10:1-11*)
Disciples known by love for others (*John 13:35*).
Disciples bear fruit as proof (*John 15:8*).
Disciplined by God (*Hebrews 12:5-11*)
Disciplined by parents (*Proverbs 19:18; 23:13*)
In the church in regard to those who sin (*1 Corinthians 5; 1 Timothy 5:20*).
Of restoring one to fellowship (*2 Corinthians 2:6-11; Galatians 6:1*)
Of warning the unruly (*1 Timothy 6:4-5*)
Of dealing with false teachers (*1 Timothy 6:3*)
Chastisement/training by the Lord (*Hebrews 12:11*)
For those God loves (*Hebrews 12:6*)
Such chastisement should not be despised (*Proverbs 3:11*).
Chiding of the Israelites by Moses (*Exodus 17:2*)
Of the Lord (*Psalm 103:9*)
By and towards Martha (*Luke 10:38-42*)

Reproof provides understanding (*Proverbs 15:32*).
Results in wisdom (*Proverbs 29:15*)
In teaching (*2 Timothy 4:2*)
In Christian love (*Revelation 3:19*)
In discipline (*Hebrews 12:5*)

23) Our oneness in Christ does not destroy our individuality. The Holy Spirit has given each Christian special gifts for building up the

Church. Now that we have these gifts, it is crucial to use them. Are you spiritually mature, exercising the gifts God has given you? If you know what your gifts are, look for opportunities to serve. If you don't know, ask God to show you, perhaps helping your minister or Christian friends. Then, as you begin to recognize your special area of service, use your gifts to strengthen and encourage the Church.

24) *Genesis 3* shows us Adam and Eve's sin separated them from the tree of life and thus kept them from obtaining eternal life. Interestingly, the tree of life again appears in a description in *Revelation 22* of people enjoying eternal life with God.

Why would the nations need to be healed if all evil is gone? John in Revelation is quoting from *Ezekiel 47:12*, where water flowing from the temple produces trees with healing leaves. He is not implying that there will be illness in the new earth; He is emphasizing that the water of life produces health and strength wherever it flows.

25) The book of Hebrews links God's saving power with His creative power. In other words, the power that brought the universe into being and that keeps it operating is the very power that removes (provides purification for) our sins. How mistaken we would be to ever think that God couldn't forgive us. No sin is too big for the Ruler of the universe to handle. He can and will forgive us when we come to Him through His Son. Jesus sitting down in heaven means that the work of redemption is complete. Christ's sacrifice was final.

26) Jesus used the image of carrying a cross to illustrate the ultimate submission required of His followers. He is not against pleasure, nor was He saying that we should seek pain needlessly. Jesus was talking about the heroic effort needed to follow Him moment by moment, to do His will even when the work is difficult and the future looks bleak. Christ knows better than we do what real life is about. He asks for submission, not self-hatred; He asked us only to lose our self-centered determination to be in charge.

27) God judges our hearts as well as our deeds, for it is in the heart that our real allegiance lies. Be just as concerned about your

attitudes that people don't see as about your actions that are seen by all.

28) Jesus' death is a beginning, not an end. Alpha and Omega are the first and last letters of the Greek alphabet. The Lord God is the beginning and the end. God the Father is the eternal Lord and ruler of the past, present, and future, for without Him you have nothing that is eternal, nothing that can change your life, nothing that can save you from sin. Is the Lord your reason for living, the Alpha and the Omega of your life? Honor the one who is the beginning and the end of all existence, wisdom, and power.

29) How can you be sure that you belong to Christ? The passage in *1 John 2:4* gives two ways to know if you do what Christ says and live as Christ wants. What does Christ tell us to do? John answers in *1 John 3:23*, "To believe in the name of His Son Jesus Christ, and to love one another." True Christian faith results in loving behavior that is why John says that the way we act can give us assurance that we belong to Christ.

30) A wise person is a model of a meaningful life. Like a tree attracts people to its shade, a person's sense of purpose attracts others who want to know how they, too, can find meaning. Gaining wisdom yourself then, can be the first step in leading people to God. Leading people to God is important because it keeps us in touch with God. Leading people to God is important because it keeps us in touch with God while offering others eternal life.

31) The sword is the only weapon of offense in the full armor of God listed in *Ephesians 6*. There are times when we need to take the offensive against Satan, and when we are tempted, we need to trust in the truth of God's Word.

32) It would certainly be a surprise if you planted corn and pumpkins came up. It's a natural law to reap what we sow. It's true in other areas too. If you gossip about your friends, you will lose their friendship. Every action has results. If you plant to please your own desires, you'll reap a crop of sorrow and evil. If you plant to please God, you'll reap joy and everlasting life. What kind of seeds are you sowing?

33) David calls us to take delight in the Lord and to commit everything we have and do to Him. But, how do we do this? To delight in someone means to experience great pleasure and joy in his or her presence. This happens only when we know that person well. Thus, "to delight in the Lord," we must know Him better. Knowledge of God's great love for us will indeed give us delight. To commit ourselves to the Lord means entrusting everything from our lives, families, jobs, and possessions to His control and guidance. To commit ourselves to the Lord means to trust in Him, believing that He can care for us better than we can ourselves. We should be willing to wait patiently for Him to work out what is best for us.

FINAL THOUGHT

You can take (eternal life) with you. The Bible says not even a lie will enter heaven. If we follow Jesus, we will take with us to heaven what Jesus taught us.

If we tell a lie or believe a lie about God, life, and spiritual matters, it will go with us to the place that has been prepared for us. It's the choice we have made of our own free will. What we hang onto is what will go with us all of our lives, and if we don't let it go, it will stay with us for eternity.

What do you want to take with you to the home of your choice? All those that love Jesus will sing in heaven with one voice. If we believe a lie we may go to hell if we do not exchange it for the truth. Satan has prepared dark, dingy cells for the unbelieving.

(**Scriptural References:** *1 Corinthians 15:1-58; Revelation 20:10*)

CPSIA information can be obtained
at www.ICGtesting.com
Printed in the USA
JSHW020027150422
24841JS00004B/91